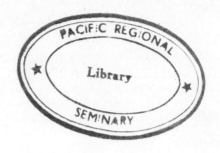

HUMAN VALUES
AND CHRISTIAN MORALITY

HUMAN VALUES AND CHRISTIAN MORALITY

JOSEF FUCHS S.J.

3136
GILL AND MACMILLAN

Published by
Gill and Macmillan Ltd
2 Belvedere Place
Dublin 1
and in London
through association with
Macmillan and Co. Ltd

Translated from the German by M. H. Heelan, Maeve McRedmond, Erika Young and Gerard Watson

Imprimi potest: Hervé Carrier, S.J., Rector Pont. Universitatis Gregorianae, Romae, die 17 Novembris 1969

Nihil Obstat
  Eduardus Gallen
  Censor Theol. Deput.

Imprimi Potest
  +Johannes Carolus
  Archiep. Dublinen.
  Hibernae Primas
Dublini die 26 Februarii anno 1970

7171 0269 6

Cover design by Des Fitzgerald

Printed and bound in the Republic of Ireland by
CAHILL & CO. LIMITED
Parkgate Street, Dublin 8

Contents

v

Preface

In the Decree on Priestly Formation (*Optatam totius*)[1] the Second Vatican Council called for a thorough renewal of moral theology; this was to be above all emphatically Christian. The summary of Christian moral theology given in this Decree presents a short and authoritative affirmation of efforts in the theological field over the previous thirty years directed towards an intensified Christianizing of moral theology. It should not be overlooked that in the Pastoral Constitution of the same Council on the Church in the Modern World (*Gaudium et spes*) a different stress and trend appear. This trend is not incompatible with that towards Christianizing moral theology, but counteracts—indeed under the influence of distinct elements of a legitimate movement towards secularization—a Christianizing movement that is one-sided and pushing ahead in the wrong direction. From its opposing standpoint it stresses the Christian's task in the world and the relative independence of the world of mankind. Thus the problem of the 'humanity' (natural moral law) of Christian morality presents itself in a new form and likewise the question of the specific 'Christianity' of the 'human' morality of the Christian.

In 1966 the writer produced a detailed commentary on this demand by the Council for an intensified Christianizing of moral theology. This first appeared as an article in a review[2] and then—together with two related essays—in book

[1]Art. 16.
[2]'Theologia moralis perficienda; votum Concilii Vaticani II', in *Periodica de re morali, canonica, liturgica* (55) 1966, 499–548.

form and in several languages. Other more recent contributions have been added to this present English language publication. They all pertain to the realm of 'fundamental morality'. The individual articles were of independent origin and are here reproduced substantially unaltered. This explains both certain repetitions and constantly evident renewed reflection on the same basic questions; and thus the date of its first appearance accompanies each article.

1 Moral Theology
According to Vatican II[1]

'Special attention needs to be given to the development of
moral theology.' So runs an injunction of the Council
Fathers in the Decree of the Second Vatican Council on
Priestly Formation.[1a] The reason for this injunction is
certainly not the pre-eminence of moral theology over the
other theological disciplines. Indeed the Council recognizes
the fundamental importance of *dogmatic* theology for moral

---

[1]Article, 'Theologia moralis perficienda; votum Concilii Vaticani II', in
Periodica de re morali, canonica, liturgica (55) 1966, 499–548.

[1a]'Under the light of faith and with the guidance of the Church's teaching
authority, theology should be taught in such a way that students will accurately
draw Catholic doctrine from divine revelation, understand that doctrine
profoundly, nourish their own spiritual lives with it, and be able to proclaim it,
unfold it, and defend it in their priestly ministry. In the study of sacred
Scripture, which ought to be the soul of all theology, students should be
trained with special diligence. . . .

'[In dogmatic theology] students should learn to penetrate the mysteries of
salvation more deeply with the help of speculative reason exercised under the
tutelage of St Thomas. They should learn too how these mysteries are inter-
connected and be taught to recognize their presence and activity in liturgical
actions and in the whole life of the Church. Let them learn to search for
solutions to human problems with the light of revelation, to apply eternal
truths to the changing conditions of human affairs and to communicate such
truths in a manner suited to contemporary man.

'Other theological disciplines should also be renewed by livelier contact
with the mystery of Christ and the history of salvation. *Special attention needs
to be given to the development of moral theology. Its scientific exposition should be more
thoroughly nourished by scriptural teaching. It should show the nobility of the Christian
vocation of the faithful, and their obligation to bring forth fruit in charity for the life
of the world. . . .*' (The Documents of Vatican II, ed. W. M. Abbott, London
1966, 451–2.)

theology and is at pains to point out that the many and
various problems of humanity find their solution in the light
of the revealed eternal truths expounded by dogmatic
theology. Moreover, the Council expressly states that study
of the Bible ought to be the very soul of all theology and
insists, in the interest of all theological disciplines, on the
necessity for a particularly careful initiation of theological
students into the study of holy Writ.

The emphatic admonition of the Council Fathers to pay
particular attention to moral theology must, therefore, be
attributed to other reasons. In the first place, moral theology
stands in a specially close relation to dogmatic theology and
occupies a specially important position among the other
theological disciplines. But a second, and more compelling,
reason is that the presentation of moral theology in the past
has left much to be desired.

The Council requires, above all, that moral theology—and
the other theological disciplines—shall be renewed through
a more lively attitude to the mystery of Christ and the history
of salvation. Students must learn to penetrate these mysteries
more deeply and to reach a livelier understanding of them
by studying holy Scripture and pondering them. They must
be recognized and experienced as a living reality, an active
force, in the life and liturgy of the Church, and as a source
for the solution of human problems. Moral theology must be
a genuine theological discipline, drawing its doctrine from
divine revelation and expounding it in the light of faith and
under the guidance of the Church's magisterium. The
Council does not want moral theology to be merely an
abstract system: it must be a body of doctrine that nourishes
the spiritual life of the students and furnishes a foundation for
the pastoral work of the priesthood.

In order that its demand for the development of moral
theology may be rightly understood and acted upon, the
Council has defined the goal of this theological discipline in
the clearest terms. The scientific exposition of moral theology,
nourished more fully on the teaching of the Bible, should

shed light upon the nobility of the vocation of the faithful in Christ and the obligation that is theirs 'to bring forth fruit in charity for the life of the world'.

In the following pages we shall endeavour to explain:

(1) how moral theology is primarily concerned with 'the exalted vocation of the faithful in Christ' and

(2) the obligation 'to bring forth fruit in charity for the life of the world';

(3) how the exposition of moral theology should be nourished on the teaching of the Bible, and

(4) planned scientifically; and

(5) how shortcomings in the traditional method of teaching can be rectified.

I. THE BASIC TRUTH: THE EXALTED VOCATION OF THE FAITHFUL IN CHRIST

The Council requires that moral theology shall be taught not only and not primarily as a code of moral principles and precepts. It must be presented as an unfolding, a revelation and explanation, of the joyful message, the good news, of Christ's call to us, of the vocation of believers in Christ. This means that

Christ and our being-in-Christ are to be its centre and focus;

the fundamental characteristic of Christian morality is a *call*, a vocation, rather than a *law*;

Christian morality is, therefore, *responsive* in character;

it is a morality *for Christians*;

its *exalted nature* must be made clear in the manner of its presentation.

We shall consider each of these five points separately.

Christ as the centre

When the Second Vatican Council made the person of Christ the centre of moral theology it certainly had no intention of excluding from that discipline all consideration of man and the morality peculiar to mankind—'natural law'. That God is the goal and end of man and therefore the ultimate basis of moral norm and obligation has to be accepted not only as a philosophical, but also as a theological, truth. On this point St Paul (*Rom.* 1:18–23) and the First Vatican Council (Denz.-Schönm 3044, 3026) leave us in no doubt. While this truth also expresses a fundamental truth of moral theology, it is, as it stands, much too abstract and inadequate. It should have a place in moral theology consonant with its fundamental importance. But it must be made quite plain that this particular truth involves only *one* element in the full and rich relationship between God and man-subsisting-in-Christ. When the Second Vatican Council wants moral theology to be centred on the person of Christ, its first and foremost concern is that the *fullness and richness* of the relationship between God and 'man-in-Christ' shall be adequately brought out. This desire of the Council is in keeping with holy Scripture.

We find this confirmed in St Paul. The apostle regards man not merely as a human creature bound because he is man to submit to God. Man, in St Paul's view, is *sinful* man whom God, through Christ, reconciled to himself (2 *Cor.* 5:18). Therefore man's submission to God as his Creator and last end comes about only through man's acceptance of the proffered reconciliation: 'Be reconciled to God' (2 *Cor.* 5:20). By this St Paul means that man must 'live for God' (cf. *Rom.* 6:11) or 'walk in newness of life' (*Rom.* 6:4), the new life which the dead and risen Christ offers us. 'Because . . . one has died for all; therefore all have died. And he died for all, that those who live might live no longer for themselves but for him who for their sake died and was raised' (2 *Cor.* 5:14 f.). Indeed St Paul's 'Be reconciled to God' is not just a pious exhortation: his words are nothing if not urgent. 'We beseech you,' he writes, 'on behalf of Christ, be reconciled to God.' (2 *Cor.* 5:20).

The apostle displays the same Christocentric view of morality when he makes it clear that our 'divinely created and oriented being' signifies, in fact, a 'being-in-Christ' (cf., for example, 1 *Cor.* 1:30). We are not meant to live merely as *man*, but as man baptized into Christ, into his death and into his resurrection, man who, through baptism, has died to sin and awakened to 'walk in newness of life'. We are therefore to consider ourselves 'dead to sin and alive to God in Christ Jesus' (cf. *Rom.* 6:1–11). That is the true position of the Christian. Man's former state, to which we have now died through baptism, was that of 'being under the law' (*Rom.* 6:14), 'being slaves of sin' (*Rom.* 6:17), 'being carnal' (*Rom.* 7:14). Our new state, on the contrary, which began with baptism, is depicted as 'being under grace' (*Rom.* 6:14), 'being "slaves" of righteousness' (*Rom.* 6:18), 'being in the Spirit' (*Rom.* 7:6; 8:2 ff.), or as possessing the Spirit of Christ who brings life (*Rom.* 8:2) and is active within us (*Rom.* 8:14–16). The norm of our morality is accordingly based on our Christian and sacramental being. The apostle, in fact, applies the principle that (natural) human behaviour derives from man's natural 'being' whereas Christian living derives from man's (supernatural) 'being-in-Christ'. In any case, what the apostle says of man's sacramental being as the ground of the Christian moral norm is applicable analogously to the *other sacraments* as well as to baptism.

In his letter to the Colossians also, the apostle of the Gentiles shows that he considers Christian morality to be based on the person of Christ. Christ is 'the first-born of all creation . . . all things were created through him and for him . . . in him all things hold together' (*Col.* 1:15–17). Christ is, at the same time, 'the first-born from the dead'. In him all the fullness of God dwells, so that in everything he may be pre-eminent (*Col.* 1:18–20). Christ is, therefore, the proto-type to whose pattern we are all created and must all conform—and this applies to our 'natural' being as well as to that special being through which we are awakened with Christ to the life of the children of God. In Christ, too, all of us actually form a sort of social entity in so far as Christ is, by God's eternal decree, 'the first-born among many brethren' (*Rom.* 8: 29). Hence, in accordance with the principle that human behaviour derives from man's 'being', it follows that not only must all of us be brought to see that the person of Christ is a pattern for every one of us, but all of us collectively must regard ourselves as forming a brotherly community and make the brotherhood a reality by active participation. Whoever is concerned to lead a truly Christian life, when he participates in this way, reveals the reality, the life, of Christ, who is the first-born of all.

In addition, St Paul regards all Christians and himself as *imitators* of Christ. Christ has come into human history and made himself an example for all to see (*Phil.* 2:7 f.; *Rom.* 15:1–7). He now lives again in glory as an example to us (cf. *Rom.* 6:1–11 and many other passages). Likewise the apostles Peter and John (1 *Pet.* 2:21; 1 *John* 2: 6) regard the life of Christ as an example for the life of Christians. And what is more, Christ himself insists that we must take the events of his life as examples for ours—things, for instance, like the washing of the disciples' feet (*John* 13:12–15) and his teaching on the love of God and of our brethren (*John* 15: 10, 13: 34). Therefore Christian life is misconceived if it is not seen as an *imitation* of the example of Christ in history and of Christ glorified. But imitation does not imply simple repetition: the Christian must relate his own individuality and situation to those of the person of Christ, and—in the circumstances of his own life—strive to bring his conduct into harmony with that of Christ.

But there is another and richer scriptural idea which, in fact, includes those just examined: the idea of personally *following* Christ. It is Christ's own idea: he called on various individuals in various ways to follow him (*Mark* 1:16–20, 2:14, 3:13; *John* 12:26, etc.). To follow Christ does not mean exclusively to be in Christ's company, to be in actual contact with him. It means rather to have a share in the living reality that is Christ, and above all to share in the fellowship of the Christian communion that puts its trust in Christ for eschatological salvation and hopes for the Parousia

(*Mark* 10: 17 f.; *John* 12:26, etc.). This idea of following Christ by giving ourselves to him includes the following of Christ's example: it gives us a deeper and fuller understanding of what Christian living ought to be, and a better grasp of moral and religious values, all of which we can make a living reality in our own lives.

Although holy Scripture in various ways points to Christ as the centre of Christian life and morality, the Council thinks it well to bring this specially to the notice of moral theologians. It is not surprising, then, that this highly important truth is also stressed or implied, in one way or another, in other Council documents. The Dogmatic Constitution on the Church (arts. 6 f.) invites us to pattern ourselves on Christ and especially to imitate his love and humility (art. 42); we are to realize that the poor, the infirm and the oppressed are united with Christ in a very special way (art. 41); members of religious orders are called upon to imitate Christ in a special way (arts. 43, 47). The following of Christ, as proposed by the gospel, should be the supreme law of the life of religious (Religious Life 2).[2] Missionaries, by their Christ-like conduct, are to make Christ's person manifest to men (Missions 24). Priests, too, live and work in accordance with the example of the High Priest, Jesus Christ (Priests 8). Finally, be it noted, the Council, frequently and in various documents, alludes to the holy Spirit as the Spirit of Christ who prompts and guides individual believers in ordering their lives in Christ's service.

It remains to point out that, when the Council places Christ in the centre of moral theology it views him in thoroughly scriptural light—as the God-*man*. Moral theology, therefore, conformably to the Council's wishes, is not to abstract from man. By doing so it becomes a supernatural

---

[2]Translator's note: The Conciliar documents will be usually referred to hereafter by keywords, followed by the article number, thus:

(Religious Life 2) = (Decree on Renewal of the Religious Life, art. 2).
(Church 11)   = (Dogmatic Constitution on the Church, art. 11).
(Priests 8)   = (Decree on the Ministry and Life of Priests, art. 8).

abstraction. It must be a moral theology of *man* and, as such, must include the moral 'law of nature'. But it must be borne in mind that moral theology does not treat of man in the raw, so to speak, but of Christian man, of man called by God 'in Christ'.

Vocation of the faithful in Christ

The Council does not commend a moral theology that is designed primarily as a code of precepts and obligations imposed upon the Christian. The presentation of moral principles in such a way degenerates all too easily into an impersonal and minimalist ethical system, not altogether secular, perhaps, but certainly much too neutral. Nor does the Council look with a more favourable eye on that type of moral theology which evolved into 'Christian ethics' in the age of rationalism and viewed Christ mainly as a moralist, albeit a truly sublime one. On the contrary, the primary task of moral theology, according to the letter and spirit of the Council, must be to explain that man is called personally in Christ by the personal God. Being called in Christ by God is certainly thoroughly personal: it is a personal communication from God to man. Hence our being called in Christ is, in the first place, a superlative gift on God's part—the gift of God's grace. And it commits us absolutely to the faithful observance of certain precepts and laws.

The calling of man in Christ means, above all, calling man to salvation. But it implies, at the same time, a life conformable to salvation, a life actuated by that perfect love which characterized the life of Christ, and it obviously implies also those Christian activities through which each of us, according to his situation, strives for perfection in Christ. In these circumstances it is easy to see that much of moral theology as it has been presented hitherto turns out to be quite secondary to its main purpose—which should be to explain the nature of man's vocation in Christ. Perhaps it would be better to say that much that is also pertinent to man's high vocation in Christ loses its wealth of meaning when considered in the abstract and not in the light of his vocation in Christ.

The word 'vocation' is more familiar to us when we use it to denote the pre-eminence of the divine call to the priest-hood (Training for the Priesthood 8), or of the special vocation that God inspires in the hearts of those he calls to be missionaries (Missions 23 f.), or of the vocation of those who, under the inspiration of the holy Spirit, enter religious orders, there to live according to the evangelical counsels (Church 43, 39; Religious Life 5).

The same concept of 'vocation' occurs in passages of the Council documents concerned with the laity and their apostolate. The laity have their own particular vocation; in their place in the world 'they are called by God'; their 'Christian vocation' is 'a vocation to the apostolate'; they are all 'called to sanctity'; they have 'a vocation to perfection in Christ' (Church 31, 32, 34; Lay Apostolate 2). And this is said not only of the laity as such but of all the faithful, for it is they that constitute the People of God. We must also note that the Dogmatic Constitution on the Church includes a special chapter (II) on 'The Call of the Whole Church to Holiness'. This call to all the faithful is to be taken in the strict sense, that is, as a call addressed by God to each member of the faithful personally. Each is called to perfect holiness (Church 11), to the perfection of charity (*ibid.* 39), to the fullness of the Christian life (*ibid.* 40). This call goes out to every one according to his rank and station (*ibid.* 39), according to his gifts and duties and the strength he has received as a gift from Christ, always under the inspiration of the holy Spirit (*ibid.* 40, 41), who allots his gifts to everyone according as he wills (*ibid.* 12). But because everyone is called individually and personally to perfection in the way proper to him, bishops and priests are exhorted to help the faithful to recognize their own divine vocation (Bishops 15; Priests 6). Lastly the Council points out that not only the faithful, but all men, are called to salvation. And this does not merely refer to the objective destination of the human race as a whole: it refers also to the existential vocation of every individual member of it by the grace of God (Church 13; Missions 2).

It is no wonder then that the Council, anxious to keep closely to the terms of holy Scripture, clings to the idea of 'calling'. To speak of God who calls and of man who is called by God is one of the more familiar biblical idioms. For the sake of brevity we will pass over the Old Testament accounts in which God is said to call his people, and also the historical fact that Christ the Lord called the disciples. St Paul frequently speaks of his apostolate as undertaken in response to a personal call by God (cf. *Rom.* 1:1; 1 *Cor.* 1:1, etc.) and generalizes this when he says, 'One does not take the honour [of priesthood] upon himself, but he is called by God' (cf. *Heb.* 5:4). He refers also to God's freedom to call whom he pleases (*Rom.* 4:17) and to call those he has predestined to fulfil their destiny (*Rom.* 8:30).

Christians are aware of their calling in Christ (cf. *Rom.* 1: 6; 1 *Cor.* 1: 9; *Eph.* 1:12). They know they have been called through the grace of Christ (*Gal.* 1: 6, 15), called to Christian freedom (*Gal.* 5:13) and called to holiness (cf. *Rom.* 1: 7, 8: 28; 1 *Cor.* 1: 2, etc.). And not alone are they aware of their high vocation, they are also conscious of the exacting nature of its morality. When Paul tells them they *are* Christians, 'saints' and free men, he means they *must be* all these things: the Pauline indicative is the imperative of the divine call. Hence the moral character of God's demand is made clear: they are to lead a life worthy of the calling to which they have been called by God (*Eph.* 4:1) and its corollary 'God has not called us for uncleanness, but in holiness' (1 *Thess.* 4:7). The Christian vocation must be given concrete expression in every Christian life, taking on different external forms in accordance with the specific gifts and status of each individual (1 *Cor.* 7:7, 17, 20 ff., 24). These are only a few out of the many examples which show that the New Testament views the perfect life to be practised by every Christian as a very lofty and highly personal vocation. It is at once God's most personal gift of grace and

his most personal claim upon us. It makes itself felt slowly but progressively as we go about our ordinary, everyday affairs.

Because the divine call is implemented in this fashion in our entirely concrete and matter-of-fact daily lives, it comprises within its scope all universal or general laws whether natural or supernatural. Being God's call to each of us, it includes the many and various internal and external conditions common to the generality of mankind and also the conditions that are peculiar to each individual among us. But although vocation in Christ embraces everything that binds the faithful as a whole and as individuals, it is not primarily directed towards these obligations but towards Christian perfection, towards self-surrender of the whole person of the Christian to Christ, towards that charity, that love, which is developed and displayed in many inward and outward manifestations in our daily lives. In other words, while our vocation in Christ certainly requires us to comply with general laws and individual obligations, it insists far more—most of all indeed—that we make room for the Spirit who, as he wills, prompts us to do all these things and more than these, but especially to progress in patterning our lives on that of our divine Master.

Moral theology must, of course, teach everything that goes to the making of a Christ-like life—obligations deriving from general principles and obligations arising from claims on particular individuals. But that is no reason why it should assume the character of a hide-bound collection of laws and of neutral and impersonal obligations—as if literal observance of such obligations was all that was needed to make a good Christian! A moral theology that takes serious account of the meaning of 'vocation in Christ' must certainly display some of the dynamism that belongs to the insistence of God's call to us, to the grace of the ever-active holy Spirit within us, to the unending pursuit of a perfection we never fully achieve, and to the love that can never be adequately expressed and never sufficiently satisfied. A dynamic moral theology will not be only an encyclopedia of laws; it will also teach us that

we are all individually called to ever greater heights of
maturity and fulfilment and—since weakness of faith and
lack of charity are never entirely absent from Christian
experience—we are called to *conversion* also. The importance
this maturity, fulfilment and conversion have for the more
intensive and profound realization of the Christian pattern
of life must be well driven home.

What we have said above is not to be taken to mean that
moral theology is dispensed from teaching all the moral
principles, laws and precepts: it means that their significance
and place within Christian morality must be clearly
indicated. Otherwise we shall have a moral theology of laws
and not a moral theology of our vocation in Christ.

Christian morality as personal response

The terms 'vocation' and 'call' suggest the responsive
character of Christian morality. Response is something more
than dialogue. The term 'responsive' conveys that it is God
who takes the initiative. He calls us and he has loved us first
(cf. 1 *John* 4:10), and we personally respond to his call by
the quality of our lives. In this way a constant dialogue goes
on between God and ourselves. At every instant and in every
situation he lovingly confronts us with ourselves and calls us
to himself. We should accept lovingly and give ourselves to
him. Even the universal moral laws serve this interpersonal
responsive morality: they turn out to be nothing other than
the abstract expression of God's will, of God's call to us. We
must be ready to respond to it with obedience. In any
concrete situation it becomes an obligation incumbent upon
all of us or a personal call to each one of us. We freely respond
by doing what it requires of us.

Clearly this responsive dialogue between God and ourselves is a dialogue that concerns salvation. Whatever God
calls us to is always a means whereby we are called to
salvation in Christ. Likewise the actions by which we respond
to God's call are oriented towards the salvation we are asked
to accept from Christ.

This concept of Christian morality as a dialogue, a morality of response, seems to make it desirable that the faithful should be conscious of, or should deliberately advert to, the responsive character of their moral conduct. This is not to say that our moral conduct lacks responsiveness if we do not reflexively advert to its responsive character.[3] Indeed, since it seems that the individual is always conscious somehow—although not reflexively—of the responsive nature of his moral conduct, we may also assume that he is always conscious of the divine call to salvation—although he does not expressly advert to it. This divine grace (we may call it that) appears to characterize every moral call from God to man.[4]

From all this we can see how great a contrast Christian moral theology presents to those systems which only just cover bare compliance with a set of moral principles.

A morality for Christians

It follows from what we have said that the morality which the Council wants taught in seminaries for the priesthood is not simply one or other of the various systems of moral philosophy, at choice, but the particular system appropriate to those who hold to the Christian faith and sacraments. *Their* moral theology must explain and illustrate their high vocation in Christ, what it implies in general and the forms it takes in practice. By Christians here we mean, primarily, Catholics. But the same call of Christ to Christian living holds good, of course, for Christians who do not see eye to eye with us in everything. We need not object if some of them

---

[3]See K. Rahner, 'Atheismus', *Lexikon für Theologie und Kirche*, I, Freiburg 1957, 983–9 especially 987–8. Also his *Theological Investigations*, III, (tr. K. H. and B. Krüger), London 1967, 239 f.; *ibid.*, V, (tr. K. H. Krüger), London 1966; *ibid.*, VI, (tr. K. H. Krüger), London 1969, 218–30; J. B. Lotz, 'Akt', *Lexikon für Theologie und Kirche*, I, Freiburg 1957, 247, 251; J. B. Metz, 'Akt, religiöser', *ibid.*, 256–9.

[4]See previous note. Also K. Rahner, *Theological Investigations*, IV, (tr. K. Smythe), London 1966. As regards knowledge of vocation and salvation, see particularly K. Rahner, *Mission and Grace*, I, (tr. C. Hastings), London 1963, 130–1; O. Semmelroth, 'Heilsnotwendigkeit', *Lexikon für Theologie und Kirche*, V, Freiburg 1960, 162 f.; A Röper, *Die anonymen Christen*, Mainz 1963.

interpret the Christian call rather differently: on particular issues they have other moral norms than ours, especially in matters which we reckon to come under the natural moral law. A renewal of moral theology on these lines would have the happy result that the morality which the Council requires to be taught to Catholic theological students would also be that recognized by Christians of other persuasions.

Non-Christians, on the other hand, present rather a problem. Their moral systems seem so very different from that with which the Council Fathers are concerned. As a matter of fact moral theologians not infrequently divide the domain of morality into two spheres, the Christian and the non-Christian, the latter being regarded as 'natural law morality'. This distinction, however, calls for substantial qualifications; it might, indeed, be better if it were dropped entirely. In fact, the morality that the Council describes as the exalted vocation in Christ appears to be the one and only morality appointed for all humanity without distinction: man, according to God's decree, is simply and solely man called in Christ. It is merely incidental that not all of mankind know and accept the divine call with the same explicitness. If we consider this, not subjectively from the viewpoint of our own knowledge, but objectively as part of the ordering of things by God's providence, we can get little satisfaction from the familiar theory that Christians have ready to hand the moral elements which non-Christians have to discover for themselves (and then only incompletely). This theory may be formally unimpeachable but it would be better to say that non-Christians largely share Christian morality, and this is true despite the fact that Christian morality contains 'supernatural' as well as 'natural' elements, since its prototype is the God-man Christ. And it cannot be objected that non-Christians have, so to speak, no right to Christian morality on such terms, for all mankind are rightful heirs to it. Moreover, there is good Catholic authority for saying that non-Christians share more than the 'natural' elements of the Christian vocation. And it cannot be presumed that non-Christians are incapable of perceiving the grace of Christ: its insistent prompting can affect their moral outlook. Nor is it impossible for non-Christians to receive—at least virtually—the supernatural Christian revelation, through the intervention of God's grace (cf. Church 8, 16; Missions 3; Pastoral Constitution 22). Indeed there are many grounds for supposing that even those who in all sincerity declare themselves atheists may encounter God, on occasion, in their inmost consciousness. They would not, of course, be reflexively conscious of any such experience.

The task of the moral theologian

The Council stresses the exalted nature of the Christian vocation. This should surely be sufficient to indicate that the right method of teaching Christian moral theology must arouse in students the conviction that the Christian moral message is a joyful one like the whole of the Christian gospel. In other words, to conform to the spirit of the Council Christian morality must be presented in such fullness that it is readily apprehended as a message that brings us joy, a message that we accept gladly. If Christian morality is rightly viewed, that is, if it is seen as centred on the person of Christ and on God's call to man in Christ, its exalted character cannot fail to be grasped and lovingly accepted. Moreover, when the students who are fortunate enough to have moral theology taught to them in this way, eventually become priests, they, in turn, will be able to present Christian morality to the faithful as a truly joyful message. They will no longer need to have recourse to mere moralizing or monotonous insistence on the obligatory nature of the divine demands. And they will then be more likely to attract their hearers instead of repelling them!

II. THE BASIC DUTY: 'TO BRING FORTH FRUIT IN CHARITY FOR THE LIFE OF THE WORLD'

The high vocation of the faithful in Christ must inevitably bear its fruit in this visible world if the faithful act in accordance with that vocation. It is the function of moral theology to point out the exalted nature of this vocation and to show that

the faithful must bring forth fruit which is appropriate to that vocation;

the chief constituent of this fruit is Christian charity;

this charity is primarily concerned with 'the life of the world' in Christ and

its object is to make this world of ours a friendlier place to live in;

in this way the various social virtues, imbued with the spirit of Christian charity, will constitute the fruit of the Christian vocation.

Gift and task

The Council enjoins the faithful to rid themselves of the individualistic view of Christian life and to work earnestly for 'the life of the world'. This injunction can hardly be over-stressed. By entering actively into the affairs of everyday life the Christian can bring forth fruit in the way our Lord had in mind when he spoke of the vine-branch that always bears fruit when it is united with the vine-stock, Christ (*John* 15:2–5). Indeed the Christian is actually obliged to show, by the good he does for others, that he is living a truly Christian life. At an early stage in its proceedings the Council had decreed: 'Collectively and individually the faithful must do their part in nourishing the world with the fruits of the Spirit' (Church 38).

This idea of fruitfulness must, however, be understood in a strictly Christian sense. The primary meaning of the Christian vocation is not an obligation forced upon us but rather a gift given to us—a gift of the Spirit of Christ, who comes to dwell in us and manifests himself within us, prompting, urging and sustaining us. According to the degree in which we freely and sincerely lay ourselves open to the Spirit he will produce spiritual fruit in us. Such a conception is obviously far removed from the Pelagian or semi-Pelagian idea of fruitfulness. It is, as St Paul tells us, a truly Christian idea: 'The fruit of the Spirit is love, joy, peace, patience, kindness, goodness, faithfulness, gentleness, self-control' (*Gal.* 5:22 f.; cf. *Rom.* 6:21 f., 7:5, 8:5–18). And, as we have already seen, the idea of *obligation* is entirely compatible with this concept of fruitfulness. The idea of *compulsion* is in contrast to this.

The less freely we accept the Spirit of Christ, the more burdensome becomes the duty of doing good to our fellow-men: a reluctantly undertaken obligation assumes the character of an imposition. So long, indeed, as we are in our mortal flesh we have not yet fully and genuinely opened ourselves to the Spirit. Consequently our obligation to 'bring forth fruit' for the life of the world always gives rise to a certain feeling of resistance; obstacles and difficulties obtrude themselves upon us. Nevertheless, when we accept the Spirit of Christ—and to the extent that we do so—we shall by his power overcome these difficulties, cheerfully do what he prompts us to do, and so bring forth the fruits of his Spirit. The Council, therefore, pictures a true Christian as one who, inspired by the indwelling Spirit of Christ, joyfully and whole-heartedly brings forth fruit for the life of the world. Active participation in the life of the world, in this truly Christian way, must be regarded as the real fruit, in the Christian sense, of a freely accepted vocation in Christ.

Charity as the fruit of the Christian vocation

The fruit of the Christian vocation for the life of the world has as its primary and fundamental element a love for all mankind; this finds concrete expression in various good works. The Council, therefore, asks theologians to emphasize in their teaching that Christian charity, love for one's neighbour, is the very soul of all the works done by the faithful 'for the life of the world'. Where God is concerned, it is not enough to offer him our works only: each of us must offer his own person, too. Where man is concerned, the same

holds good. We must love God above all. We must love him
so much that our works will be tokens to prove our personal
surrender to him. We must place ourselves completely and
whole-heartedly at the disposal of the whole race of men
whom the Father has called in all that concerns their good.
What we do for them will be signs of our sincerity and
brotherly love.[5] Those that believe in Christ's good news and
respond to its message must stand out strikingly from the rest
of humanity by their love of mankind. Indeed nobody can
receive the gift of divine sonship who, in his own personal
life, loves the Father and does not love his fellow-man as
well. If he is to claim, through Christ, a share in the sonship,
he must love the Father and all mankind just as Christ
loved them (*John* 15:10; 13:34) and must, as Christ did,
give himself—even empty himself (cf. *Phil.* 2:7; *Gal.* 2:20).

That the true love of God must include love of one's
neighbour forms the basis of every exposition of our sublime
Christian vocation. We may recall the incisive words in
which St John explains the intimate connection between love
of God and love of one's fellow-men: 'If any one says, "I love
God", and hates his brother, he is a liar; for he who does not
love his brother whom he has seen, cannot love God whom
he has not seen' (1 *John* 4:20). These words of Scripture[6]
would seem to suggest that the love of God, in the explicit
and categorical sense—that is, conceived in terms of the love
of human beings for one of their number in the ordinary
human way—appears to be possible only because human
beings do, or can, love one another in the explicit and
categorical sense. The love of God, indeed, from the very
nature of its origin, does not appear to be explicit and

[5]Cf. G. Gilleman, *The Primacy of Charity in Moral Theology*, (tr. W. F. Ryan
and A. Vachon), Westminster, Maryland, U.S.A. 1959; and K. Rahner,
Theological Investigations, V (see note 3, above). Cf. also Thomas Aquinas,
S. theol. I–II, q. 108, 2c; 'Rectus autem *gratiae* usus est per opera *caritatis.*
Quae secundum quod sunt de necessitate virtutis, pertinent ad praecepta
moralia. . . .'

[6]Regarding what follows, cf. K. Rahner, 'Warum und wie können wir die
Heiligen verehren?', *Geist und Leben* (37) 1964, 325–39.

categorical, as human love is; rather is it a non-categorical love, a love that transcends the categories. This non-categorical or transcendent love, however, makes possible the explicit-categorical love of one's neighbour and so makes possible—through the medium of the latter—man's explicit-categorical love of God ('whom he has not seen') after the manner of his love for his neighbour ('whom he has seen'). The moral theologian, then, must point out that so far as Christian works 'for the life of the world' are concerned, Christ's call to us to love the Father also means that we must give nothing other and nothing less, for the life of the world, than our love for the world and for all who are in it.

The Council, too, brings out this point in its various decrees: the first and most important contribution we have to make to the life of the world is the gift of ourselves. Our love must be absolutely selfless for it will animate and inspire all other works of ours. Priests, for instance, must exercise their ministry with loving care for those committed to their charge (Priests 14). The presence of the Christian faithful in the missions is a manifestation of love for their fellow-men (Missions 12; cf. 19). The ministries of the various religious communities are said to be so many works of charity, to be discharged in the name of the Church herself (Religious Life 8). The basis and bedrock of the lay apostolate is the law of love for all men (Lay Apostolate 3); 'every exercise of the apostolate should take its origin and power from charity', from love of one's neighbour (*ibid.* 8). The power that the Church can 'inject into' the world is rooted in faith and brotherly love actively put into practice (Pastoral Constitution 42).

Christian charity and the life of the world
The life of the world, the first fruit of our Christian vocation, is evidently taken by the Council to mean the life that Christ brought into the world. For in Christ's own words he came that we may have life, and have it abundantly (*John* 10:10) and the bread he gave us is nothing other than his

flesh 'for the life of the world' (*John* 6:51). And, as Scripture tells us again and again, the life referred to here is everlasting life.

A genuinely Christian moral theology must, therefore, transcend every individualistic conception of salvation that might be satisfied with its own self-sufficient view of Christ's sublime call to us. We should not attempt to describe the Christian vocation without emphasizing that it must bear the fruit of love in union with Christ, and that the world has the life that Christ brought it and has it in full measure. Vocation in Christ gives us salvation and life. But these gifts must be shared with our fellow-men. The very nature of the gifts and the demands of brotherly love compel us to do so. They must be passed on not only to those who could receive the grace of Christ without ever having heard of him (cf. Church 13; Missions 2), but also to those who already adhere to the Christian faith. These gifts, moreover, are not to be transmitted in an indifferent or perfunctory manner but in such a way that believers and non-believers receive them ever more abundantly.

Because it is the duty of the faithful to utilize their special gifts for the life of the world, moral theology must, from the very outset, direct attention to the fact that moral conduct, even in the most private sphere, and whether it be good or bad, must never be regarded as a matter that concerns only the individual: it must always be viewed also in its social aspect.[7] In other words, moral theology must stress the importance of every individual's moral life for the true life of the world. Beyond all doubt personal morality has *social significance*. It is fraught with consequences for the People of God and for all human society, among which are the following: (1) The standard of personal morals that prevails

[7]On the social aspect see *inter alia* H. Assmann, *Die soziale Dimension der persönlichen Sünde* (manuscript Gregoriana) Rome 1960; M. Seybold, *Sozial-theologische Aspekte der Sünde bei Augustinus*, Regensburg 1963; and in particular J. Beumer, 'Die persönliche Sünde in sozial-theologischer Sicht', *Theologie und Glaube* (43), Paderborn 1953, 81–101; P. Schoonenberg, 'Zonde der wereld en erfzonde', *Bijdragen* (24), 1963, 349–86.

in any social group determines the quality of Christian life in that group and whether it is lived in all its fullness or otherwise. (2) The grace that manifests itself as charisms in individual believers becomes diffused, in some degree, throughout the People of God in that society. (3) The efficacy of the sanctifying action of the Church varies with the moral standard of its individual members. (4) This being so, the public image presented by the Church is always liable to be taken as the index of her credibility.

Personal morality, again, exerts an *influence on society*. This may be of a kind that is incapable of being empirically determined—the salvation of many, for instance, can depend on the life of grace in individuals—but it may also be of a kind that is empirically determinable, for man, being social by nature, must necessarily by his behaviour exercise an influence, and leave an impress, on his environment. Whether grace will be diffused through the various spheres of human life depends, for one thing, on the sensitivity of social behaviour to the influence of individuals in the group; but it also depends on whether grace itself is 'visible' (in its effects) and has the power to attract others. Moreover, many outward actions are obviously aimed at developing or destroying Christian living in certain persons or certain areas. The *inward* thoughts and feelings of the individual also have their effect: it is these that form the mental attitude which will determine the outward behaviour of the individual. This latter, in turn, will affect his environment and help to create within it the moral climate that will influence its members in their dealings and in their 'life', in the life that Christ wishes us to have.

Concern that man should live his life in this world in accordance with Christian ideals requires not only that we should pay attention to the social aspect of our moral conduct but also that we should busy ourselves actively with the further task of protecting and propagating the ideals of Christian living. The Council Fathers drive this home forcibly in several of their decrees. They point out that apostolic care for the life of the world is not a matter solely for those called to the apostolate in a very special way, such as bishops, priests, missionaries and religious. It is a duty imposed on the Church as a whole and it is in the name of the Church as a whole that those who have these special vocations carry on their activities. The Council stresses this particularly in the texts on the lay apostolate, whose objective is, of course, the fostering and diffusion of true Christian life throughout the world. The laity must take part in apostolic work because the Church itself is committed to it and so, therefore, are all its members. The laity are not, first and foremost, only lay people: because of their Christian vocation, they are called to the apostolate. The lay apostolate is a participation in the saving mission of the Church itself. 'Through their baptism and confirmation all are commissioned to that apostolate by the Lord himself' (Church 33; cf. Lay Apostolate 3). 'The Church carries on the apostolate in various ways through all its members. For by its very nature the Christian vocation is also a vocation to the apostolate' (Lay Apostolate 2). By their apostolic activity 'the laity share in the priestly, prophetic and royal office of Christ and therefore have their own part in the mission of the whole People of God' (*ibid.*). The obligation to bring forth fruit through the apostolate for the life of the world extends, however, in the case of bishops and priests to other works than those proper to the laity. The special function of the latter is to work for the perfection in Christ of the temporal order, of the things of this world. Different members of the laity must perform different tasks according to their various capacities, the urgency of the work to be done, and other relevant circumstances. The obligation to engage in apostolic work for the life of the world can also bind members of the Church on various other grounds. When, for example, a member of the Church discharges the functions of such-and-such an office, he must carry out his duties in a manner consistent with *justice*; or where an ecclesiastical body, let us say, is confronted with a critical situation, consideration must be given to the requirements of *social justice*; or where a spiritual emergency calls for our intervention, we intervene on the ground of Christian *charity*. But charity, the greatest of all gifts for the life of the world, animates all apostolic efforts for the salvation of others. The Council Fathers, after stating that all the laity are commissioned to the apostolate through baptism and confirmation, go on to say, in a particularly fine passage: 'The sacraments, and especially the Holy Eucharist, mediate and sustain that charity towards God and man which is the soul of the entire apostolate' (Church 33).

Charity and the world we live in

When the Council insists that moral theology must stress the obligation to bring forth fruit for the life of the world, it has dealt explicitly with only one—albeit the most important and indispensable—element in the social aspect of the Christian vocation. By this the Council did not, of course, imply that other elements of this social aspect could be ignored. As a matter of fact, they have been dealt with by the Council in the Pastoral Constitution on the Church in the Modern World, and this more than suggests that moral theology should have a hand in them too. Two points have to be considered here. In the first place, if the Christian vocation brings with it the obligation to work in charity for the *supernatural* life—for the salvation—of mankind, the full import of this obligation can hardly be grasped unless it is conceived as an obligation to work for *mankind* who are called to that supernatural life, and for the world in which they live. Secondly, it should not be forgotten that the very existence, the reality, of man and his world has a trans-cendental significance which bears on 'the life of the world'. This reality of man and his world has, to be sure, its own particular and inherent nature; but because of man's vocation in Christ it has at the same time a more profound, a transcendental, meaning.

These were, no doubt, the considerations that prompted

the Council to deal with man and his world in the Pastoral Constitution mentioned above. In this the Council asked that those who were called to be Christians should contribute for the good of man and his world what they, enlightened by their faith in Christ and inspired by his grace, were able to contribute. That Constitution, therefore, sets out the Christian view of the dignity of the human person, man's inalienable rights, the solidarity of mankind, social justice, the structures of society, marriage and the family, human culture, socio-economic life, the political community and the international family of nations. Moreover, in the Dogmatic Constitution on the Church the Council addresses the following exhortation to the laity: 'By their competence in secular fields and by their personal activity, refined and ennobled by the grace of Christ, let them work energetically so that by human labour, technical skill and civic culture created goods may be perfected for the benefit of all men, according to the design of the Creator and in the light of his Word. Let them ensure that created goods are more fittingly distributed among men and . . . lead to general progress in human and Christian liberty' (Church 36). All this requires that moral theology will have to inculcate that our lofty Christian vocation also imposes on us a concern for human and earthly realities. This, indeed, is where the faithful will have to bring forth the fruits of their vocation. And it does not exclude—in fact it takes for granted—that moral theology must in the first place treat, in the greatest possible depth, the inherent nature of these realities and, in the second place, must explain the obligation, devolving upon man by reason of his divinely ordained destiny, to actuate the possibilities of man and the world.

Christian charity and the social virtues

Charity, the greatest of all gifts for man and his world, must therefore be the soul and stimulus of our work 'for the life of the world' and it must be applied universally throughout that sphere. Needless to say, justice, mercy, generosity, truthfulness and all other virtues that make for mankind's good must always be practised. It is a great thing, for example, to stand up vigorously for social justice. Yet something more is expected from us, and that something more is Christian charity. While the great value of the other virtues, is, of course, undeniable, nevertheless they should indicate and make manifest a still greater value—charity. Certain worldly human factors enter into the exercise of the various other virtues, but in exercising charity man gives himself in person. The other virtues are therefore essentially 'mediations' of charity and they should, in fact, be required to 'mediate' it.[8] It may be that charity 'orders' or 'appoints' the ultimate object of a particular virtue or, in other words, that charity is the ground on which a particular virtue is put into practice in a concrete act. But it can also be that charity does not 'order' or 'appoint' the exercise of the other virtues but penetrates these virtuous acts in depth, and that the individual who performs them is conscious, although not reflexively conscious, of this. And so, by practising the various other virtues, we can bring forth fruit for the life of the world 'in charity'.

III. CHRISTIAN MORAL THEOLOGY IS ROOTED IN THE SCRIPTURES

The primary task of moral theology must be to demonstrate the exalted nature of our vocation in Christ and our consequent obligation 'to bring forth fruit in charity for the life of the world'. Accordingly the Council expressly requires that moral theology must above all have its roots deep in holy Scripture and grow and develop in the 'fertile soil' of scriptural teaching. This done it will become clearer that knowledge of the mystery of Christ and of the history of salvation must be the essential context of moral theology. This new emphasis on holy Scripture and on the connection

[8]On mediation see note 5 above—G. Gilleman, *op. cit.*

c

of moral theology with the mystery of Christ and the history
of salvation inevitably helps us to a better understanding of
moral theology.

The Bible and moral theology[9]

In its Decree on Training for the Priesthood (art. 16) and
particularly in the Dogmatic Constitution on Divine
Revelation (art. 24) the Council stresses that the sacred
Scriptures must be the soul of all theology. The reason for
this is not hard to find. The last-named document, in fact,
goes on to say that the sacred Scriptures express the apostolic
message in a special way. They contain the word of God and,
since they are inspired, really are the word of God (art. 24).
What the Council requires of theology in general, namely,
that it shall rest on the perpetual foundation of the word of
God—by which it will be 'most powerfully strengthened and
constantly rejuvenated' (*ibid.*)—is further emphasized in a
special reference elsewhere to the teaching of moral theology
(Training for the Priesthood 16). While we can see good
reason for all this when we view the work of past centuries, it
will be well to look more closely at some aspects of the matter.

Firstly, when the Council lays down that moral theology
should be 'more thoroughly nourished by scriptural teaching'
it does not exactly mean that the nourishment should take
the form of arguments drawn from the Bible for particular
principles and particular norms of morality. It means rather
that the fundamental orientation and conception of moral
theology should be determined by sacred Scripture. That is
quite clear from the context (vocation in Christ, etc.). It
would appear, too, that the Council had in mind not just
a scriptural moral theology but rather a basically scriptural
outlook that would guide and permeate it. In this way the
desired connection with the mystery of Christ and the history
of our salvation would be suitably effected. Whether, for

---

[9]Cf. E. Hamel, 'L'usage de l'Ecriture Sainte en théologie morale', *Gregorianum*
(47) 1966, 53–85, which, together with note 23 below, gives a detailed bibliography.

example, the starting-point would be Aristotle or the gospel, an explanation of the *philosophical* idea of 'law' would have to be given; it could be a short one if the point had already been taken up in the course on ethics or a longer one if this were not the case. But if the starting-point is holy Scripture it will not be possible to evade the *theological* problem of 'law', that is, its relation to divine love, grace and justification, and also to its unfolding as the law of Christ in salvation history. Another case in point is the Christocentric conception of Christian morals, which we briefly discussed in our first chapter. Again, we have St Paul's conception of Christian morality as the reconciliation of sinful man to God (2 *Cor.* 5:18–21), a conception, certainly, very far removed from that of Pelagius and his disciples. This reconciliation must be presented as the work of God's love for sinners but also and at the same time as a divine imperative addressed to sinners. And over and above all this, we have only to think how startlingly the idea of the perfection of man, preached by Christ in the Sermon on the Mount, or the idea of imitating or 'following' Christ, or St Paul's idea of the spiritual man, differs from the ideas of virtue and human perfection that are to be found in non-Christian moral systems!

A theology that does not draw from the scriptural source must inevitably wander away from the truth, whereas a moral theology that starts from the sacred Scriptures maintains an unmistakably Christian character. It would seem then that a presentation of moral theology on the latter lines would be particularly suitable for the formation of future priests and would be of help to them in preaching the Christian moral message. Two things, certainly, must be borne in mind. This scriptural presentation of moral theology is not just a matter of quoting a few pious, decorative texts or a few rather vague ruminations; it must include a reasoned exegesis. No more is it sufficient merely to describe or illustrate biblical trains of thought; it is often necessary to provide a thorough theological interpretation of them.

Secondly, in endeavouring to arrive at the proper scriptural orientation of moral theology we shall find that the biblical theology—especially the biblical moral theology—developed by exegetes during the last few decades is of great service. It provides an exegesis which is faithful to the text and which at the same time by comparing different texts, trains of thought and ranges of ideas, brings out the deeper meaning and historical evolution of biblical statements. In this way students will be better able to understand the modes of thought and expression peculiar to holy Scripture, and the Christian message can be taken directly from the New Testament itself.

To be sure, biblical moral theology is not identical with moral theology in the general sense of that term. For one thing the Bible is no systematic theological treatise; its theology has to be worked out, so to speak, by theologically processing the data of revelation which it gives us. And the Bible does not provide us with a tidy theoretical system, or a synthesis of the principles and precepts, of Christian morality, and it definitely does not give us the solutions of many moral problems that have arisen and are likely to arise in the course of time. The moral theologian, however, cannot burke these problems. On the other hand, a biblical theology that would confine itself exclusively to the study of the text could produce results that would have no relevance at all to Christian morals. The Old Testament books describe the moral outlook of the various periods in the history of the Israelites. A knowledge of these is indispensable for investigating the historical and spiritual development of the people called by God, through long ages, to be his own. But what directly concerns Christian morality is the moral truths revealed by the word of God; it is not the moral outlook of a people (even the chosen people), not the view of any individual sacred author, not even the positive divine law intended for a particular people such as the Israelites.

Thirdly, holy Scripture can give us not only general moral bearings but also guiding principles and even definite and concrete norms in some cases, and we should draw upon these as far as possible. But here too, a scriptural outlook will not be attained by merely distributing a few texts throughout a lesson so as to give it a biblical flavour and an edifying look. Nor can the Council's requirements be met by developing a biblical argument or two (more suited to apologetics than moral theology) or relying on a little learned exegesis of a kind, alas, that could be described as 'wishful'. Let us take an example. Scriptural proof that onanism is unlawful is not established by quoting texts which *perhaps* imply that this is so. On the contrary, if scientific exegesis finds that there is no text which furnishes absolutely certain proof of this, it must be frankly admitted that a genuine biblical proof is impossible. This also covers all cases where texts *perhaps* mean this or that (or *also* mean this or that), without our being quite certain about it. Take the question, too, of unchastity of the kind we call extra-marital intercourse; the texts which indicate that unchastity (*porneia*) is unlawful are not by themselves sufficient to prove that this is so. It must be proved that 'unchastity' has that particular meaning in a particular text. And even when it is established that what is condemned in a particular text is unchastity in the sense of extra-marital intercourse, it must still be proved whether *all* such unchastity is meant or only one form of it, for example, intercourse with a prostitute (cf. 1 *Cor.* 6:12–20). Finally it must be noted that biblical statements and condemnations in moral matters are often worded in general terms and without any qualification. On this ground *alone* there need be no hesitation in treating them as strictly general principles which admit of no exception. We must not expect biblical statements to be formulated with anything like text-book precision. Therefore we can take them as universally valid only when their wording envisages 'normal' and not exceptional cases.

Moral theology is increasingly dependent on co-operation with exegesis, but much still remains to be done in this connection. Can exegetes tell us, for example, exactly how we are to interpret exclusion from heaven on account of certain sins? We know quite well, of course, the lists of sins involved. But what we should like to know is whether exclusion follows from each single act or only from a 'grievous' act. (We have in mind, for instance, the 'dissensions' of 2 *Cor.* 12:20, *Gal.* 5:20, and *Rom.* 16:17.) Or does exclusion operate in some cases only where a habit has set in and not because of a single act? Again, what have exegetes got to say about the opinion of many Protestant theologians that certain norms in sacred Scripture must be understood not as principles and norms but only as *examples* or illustrations of the general orientation which is charity? And can exegesis help us to pronounce on the opinion of some Protestant theologians that certain norms, proposed for example, by St Paul (e.g. in the matter of homosexuality) ought not to be taken as *revealed* principles but rather as the personal views of the apostle (and of many worthy men of his day) which he expressed in order to bring out the contrast between the life of the 'spiritual', and that of the 'carnal', man?

Fourthly, the decalogue must be treated as a separate problem.[10] Much has been written in the last hundred years or so about its history, form, spirit and moral significance. There is no need to repeat it here. Indeed the Council itself makes no direct allusion to the decalogue when it speaks of holy Scripture as the fertile soil that nourishes moral theology. On the one hand, the decalogue is of outstanding importance in the unfolding of the history of salvation, the history of God's dealings with his people and it has inevitably undergone an evolution of its own. On the other hand, it was, in fact, delivered by God only to the Chosen People, as a fundamental law or constitution. For *us* it is valid because

[10]As regards the decalogue cf. P. Delhaye, *Le Décalogue et sa place dans la morale chrétienne*, Brussels 1963; E. Hamel, *Loi naturelle et loi du Christ*, Bruges 1964, 107–63, which gives a further bibliography. Also J. Schreiner, *The Commandments of God's People* (tr. M. H. Heelan), Dublin 1968; and E. Hamel, *Les dix paroles; perspectives bibliques*, Brussels-Montreal 1969.

it consists to a great extent of elements of natural or universal moral law, and especially because these elements were actually transmitted to us as valid norms in the New Testament (by Christ and St Paul). Consequently moral theology must not be satisfied with a simple appeal to the norms of the decalogue, which, after all, was the law given by God to his chosen people, the Israelites. What is more, most of the ten commandments originally had meanings quite different from those which their present interpretations would lead one to suppose. This is something that must not be forgotten in any appeal to the decalogue.

The mystery of Christ and the history of salvation in moral theology

A moral theology that draws its sustenance from the fertile soil of holy Scripture is obviously not the same as philosophical ethics. Holy Writ shows us what man's life is like when it is based on the mystery of Christ and the salvation Christ brought us. Moral theology treats of the more practical side of this life. The Council Fathers say: 'The whole training of students should be planned in the light of the mystery of salvation as it is revealed in the Scriptures' (Missions 16). In fine, the governing principle of moral theology is not man's reason but the faith through which are revealed Christ and the salvation he brings us. Moral theology explores and explains the implications of the practical side of this faith. It considers first the moral truths that have been directly revealed and then the truths that emerge from the revealed Christian mystery when the latter is examined by reason enlightened by faith. Moral theology must always be fully conscious, and must continually emphasize that it, too, is theology in the same sense as is dogmatic theology, and that it relies on reason only in so far as reason contributes to understanding and explaining faith. A large part of moral theology is taken up with the consideration of 'natural law'. But it should be made clear that reasoning from natural law has one purpose only—that of explaining more realistically, more profoundly and more completely, our life in Christ. Revelation itself, from which we draw our faith in the mystery of Christ and of our salvation, urges us as believers to do those things that man 'naturally' recognizes as worthy of man. Hence moral theology concerns itself with natural morality because of our Christian faith; natural law, in fact, belongs to the norm of life of ourselves to whom the mystery of Christ and salvation has been revealed.

Moral theology, then, whose basic aim is a better understanding of our faith, must constantly stress its relation to dogmatic theology. It is often alleged that it has gradually separated itself from dogmatic theology and become an independent discipline. In so far as this is true the bond that joined them must be restored—to a certain degree at any rate. For practical reasons moral theology and dogmatic theology are now usually taught as separate disciplines and specialization requires that this shall continue. But when, in teaching moral theology, a particular moral truth is found to be closely bound up with certain dogmatic truths, the latter must be dealt with briefly on the spot. In this way, then, moral theology can and should play its part in helping dogmatic theology to find the solutions to human problems and 'to apply eternal truths to the changing conditions of human affairs' (Training for the Priesthood 16).

All this suggests that the moral theologian should consider what can be said, in the light of revelation, on many urgent problems of our time, and what the Council actually says about them in the Pastoral Constitution on the Church in the Modern World. In that document the following are some of the most noteworthy matters dealt with: the dignity of the human person, the community of mankind and the communitarian nature of man's vocation, the theological significance of man's activity in this world and of earthly affairs in general; and marriage, the family, and culture, etc., in particular.

In addition, the moral theologian should present his subject to the student not as an abstract and autonomous branch of learning, something to be placed on a pedestal and admired, but as a branch of learning which vitally concerns him, which even shapes his own destiny. God has surely not revealed himself in order that we should lose ourselves in passive admiration of him. What he wants more than anything is to bring us to salvation.

The attempt is often made to present moral theology under some central motif such as the kingdom of God, the following or imitation of Christ, the sacramental man, the mystical body of Christ, Christian charity and so on. A moral theology grounded on the sacred Scriptures can profitably make use of an idea of this kind,[11] and thus present students with an integral and not 'merely moral' or moralistic view of human life. And it does not matter if the unifying motif is only one among several that are applicable to moral theology.

Aids to a better understanding of moral theology

Firstly, it is certain that moral theology, as the Council would like it to be, cannot be exclusively or even primarily concerned with *commandments and sins,* while the further explanation of morality and spirituality is left to another discipline—to ascetical and mystical theology as it used to be called, or 'spiritual theology' as it is often called today. Once it is realized that the primary object of moral theology is man's vocation in Christ, seen in the light of holy Writ and the saving mystery of Christ, then there can be no doubt that to confine the scope of moral theology to commandments and sins is inadmissible. This is still true even if certain moral theologians and representatives of the ascetical-mystical discipline continue to demand and defend this indefensible fragmentation of studies. It should be clear from the pronouncements of the Second Vatican Council and indeed from any calm and objective consideration of the question, that such fragmentation would mean that the subject

[11]See bibliography in note 24 below.

described as Christian morality would certainly not be *the* Christian morality but only a one-sided extract from it, an extract chosen so unhappily that it would obscure the true and lofty nature of Christian morality.

For the same reason it is also inadmissible to assign to the discipline of moral theology proper the function of establishing general principles and applying them to 'moral' cases, at the same time reserving for 'spiritual theology' instruction regarding the perfection of consciences under the personal and individual guidance of the holy Spirit. This is another case where a fundamental element of Christian morality would be excluded from moral theology and allotted to another discipline. An element of the first importance would thus be forcibly removed, so to speak, from the orbit of moral theology. There could be little objection, however, on practical grounds, if moral theology were to confine itself to giving a formal description of this element of individual guidance through the holy Spirit. In that case, it would be the task of spiritual theology to teach the concrete way and 'art' of Christian living and how the guidance of the holy Spirit can be discerned and understood.

Secondly, the Council's admonition regarding the renewal of moral theology ought to put an end to the one-sided idea prevailing in some quarters that the main object of the discipline is the training of future *confessors*.[12] Undoubtedly a moral theology primarily intended for future servants of the people of God must take serious account of the office of confessor. A moral theology for seminarians which did not deal with confessional needs—as if it considered them too practical—would not be fulfilling its proper purpose. On the other hand it would not do to teach the future priest a moral theology that tried, above all things, to be practical and failed to provide a deeper biblical and theological understanding of Christian morality. What really matters indeed is that the fullness and loftiness of Christian morality shall be

---

[12]Cf. O. Lottin, 'Morale pour chrétiens et morale pour confesseurs', *Ephemerides Theologiae Lovaniensis* (35) 1959, 410–22.

demonstrated as it emerges from holy Writ and from knowledge of the mystery of Christ and our salvation. Otherwise an essential element of the Christian moral message is kept from the future priest. As a matter of fact, many manuals of moral theology are conceived so one-sidedly as manuals for confessors that one would hardly dare to give them into the hands of Catholic lay people or of any other Christians because the sublime nature of Christian morality is scarcely recognizable from the way they present it.

The one-sidedness of these manuals of 'moral theology for confessors' is revealed by a glance through a typical one on the subject of sin. Many distinctions and explanations are given in this manual which could be equally well applied to good actions or to moral actions in general, but—character-istically—they appear only in the tract on *sin*. Take, for example, the distinction between mortal and venial sin or the differentiation of sins according to their kind and number. The latter would be valid also for good actions and moral actions generally. And, as we see more clearly every day, gradations of gravity in the moral sphere are not limited to those that distinguish mortal from venial sin.

Moreover, the so-called 'moral theology for confessors' turns out to be quite inadequate for confessors. The true Christian conversion of the penitent sinner in the sacrament of penance necessitates careful judgement and wise guidance on the confessor's part. But this supposes that the confessor has a sound understanding of the real meaning and value of Christian morality coupled with a corresponding knowledge of the laws of growth that govern man's spiritual and mental life—that is if the sacrament is to be more than a mere tribunal for giving absolution.

Thirdly, if (as the Council desires) the true meaning and excellence of Christian morality are to be made plainer to our priests-in-training, a further problem arises. Is moral theology to go on dealing with the many questions of *canon law* that have been traditionally, and are still, assigned to it? Undoubtedly moral theology must handle questions about

Christian behaviour towards ecclesiastical authority and its laws and regulations. It must also deal with questions about correct compliance with laws enacted by secular, as well as ecclesiastical, authorities. (These questions of 'special' morality should not, of course, be included in the manual of 'general' or fundamental Christian morality but preferably in that dealing with man's life in society and the social virtues.) But if, for example, the explanation of the general norms of canon law (Codex Iuris Canonici, can. 8–86) is to be included in fundamental moral theology, then it will be exceedingly difficult for the student to obtain a correct idea of the full meaning and value of Christian morality—which, after all, should be the primary purpose of the manual of fundamental moral theology. For the same reason, here even more compelling, students of moral theology should not have to study manuals of canon law dealing with ecclesiastical penalties and persons (e.g. clergy, religious and the Roman Curia); yet this not infrequently falls to their lot in present circumstances. The insertion of such matters in a curriculum of moral theology certainly indicates that such a moral theology is intended to be an introduction to the knowledge required for the exercise of the priestly office. In the process, however, the treatment of moral questions is subordinated to that aim.

Here, obviously, we can see a tendency not at all in keeping with the Council's directive for the renewal of moral theology. The insertion of so much canon law material in the moral theology course must hinder the student from getting a real grasp of the meaning and value of Christian morality. Many canonists, for their part, are also convinced that the use of canon law manuals in courses of moral theology is of no service to their own discipline.[13]

In addition, there is the separate question whether the moral theology curriculum is the proper place for a manual on the reception and administration of the *sacraments*. The

[13]Cf. *Apollinaris* (9) 1936, 215 for report of the Congress of Jurists held in Rome, 1935.

fact that instruction of this kind ever came to be included in moral theology is another indication that the latter discipline was formerly conceived more as pastoral theology than moral theology proper. There are many questions, to be sure, in the (non-dogmatic) manuals on the sacraments which are, strictly speaking, moral questions. The grounding of Christian morality on the sacraments, on the 'sacramental man', is undoubtedly a matter for moral theology, and an appropriate place can be found for it in fundamental moral theology. Again, reception of the sacraments as the right way to fulfil and to nourish the Christian's moral life is also a question of morals. On the other hand, matters involving, for example, the valid administration of the sacraments, and many of the canon law questions now treated in moral theology are not really proper to that discipline. A case in point is marriage law; other examples are jurisdiction and reservation in the administration of the sacrament of penance and the copious legislation on the sacrament of holy orders. It is worth noting, meanwhile, that many faculties and seminaries have found their own solutions of this difficulty without having to resort to excessive 'vivisection' of the material.

Our purpose in all this should now be clear. The presentation of moral theology to students must not be impeded too much by elements that are more or less extraneous to that discipline as the Council understands it. The Council requires that moral theology shall be imbued with a deeper sense of Christian living by constant contact with sacred Scripture and the knowledge of the mystery of Christ and the salvation of man that Scripture gives us. The faithful will then become more conscious of their high vocation in Christ and of the obligations that arise from it.

IV. THE SCIENTIFIC CHARACTER OF MORAL THEOLOGY

The description of moral theology in the Council's Decree on Training for the Priesthood could give rise to a misunderstanding: it could be taken as a suggestion that moral theology should cultivate a rather affective approach to Christian morality and develop a preachy, 'pious' method of presenting it to the student. The Council, no doubt, foresaw this possibility and to counter it stipulated that there must be a 'scientific exposition' of moral theology. Much could be said about this requirement but it may suffice here if we confine ourselves to the points arising under the following heads:

The Council undoubtedly requires more than a merely 'kerygmatic' exposition of Christian morality;

it also requires more than a purely casuist one.

The scientific exposition of moral theology demands a commensurate examination of the data of theological, philosophical and psychological anthropology and

a corresponding confrontation with other moral theories, Christian and non-Christian;

it must endeavour to overcome the difficulties that arise from the relation between moral theology, ethics and dogmatics.

It is especially important that the scientific character of moral theology shall be fostered by the theological faculties.

Moral theology and kerygma

It is essential that those who are brought into contact with moral theology shall realize that it is concerned with the joyful message, the 'good news', of Christ. They must get the opportunity to understand, appreciate and experience its intrinsic value and to recognize that the solutions offered by moral theology constitute a genuine attempt to attack and overcome the real problems of humanity. It must be brought home to them that the manner in which moral theology is presented, its 'image', will have a profound influence on those who come after them and on those to whom they will preach and minister when they enter upon their pastoral work. A completely abstract and detached mode of thought and teaching is not the proper medium for a moral theology that would fulfil the requirements we have mentioned.

On the other hand, the influence of moral theology on the formation of Christian attitudes will not be furthered by a 'pious' or preachy presentation of the subject. This influence must be determined by deeper insight into the truth itself. In moral, no less than in dogmatic, theology truth must be sought out and presented in a way that will be scientific without being too abstract and detached from life.

For an adequate scientific exposition of moral theology the following are the essential requirements:

(1) A use of holy Scripture enriched by acquaintance with contemporary scientific exegesis as regards the truths pertaining to Christian living.

(2) A sound knowledge of the moral ideas that have taken shape over the centuries since the rise of Christianity. How important this is can be seen from the ideas put forward in the contemporary scientific discussion of married life and sexuality in general.

(3) A knowledge of the traditional doctrine that continues to be held by the Church regarding certain moral matters. To establish the truth of this doctrine it would be necessary, apart from being familiar with the tradition, to form a judgement on its value so far as contemporary fundamental theology can furnish adequate criteria for forming such a judgement.

(4) An accurate knowledge, interpretation and appraisal of the official pronouncements of the Church's magisterium —of the Pope and the other bishops. Here, too, the criteria for interpretation and appraisal offered by fundamental theology have to be taken into account. Documents issued by the magisterium will have to be assembled and produced in class. But this is not all: consideration of the relevant

criteria for the interpretation and appraisal of the documents will very definitely be no light task.

(5) A profound insight into holy Scripture and tradition, both of which must be examined theologically in order to reach a deeper understanding of revealed truths. In addition there must be a genuine, objective discussion—and not merely an apologetical one—of the truths of natural law in order to arrive at soundly understood principles and conclusions. And the scientific nature of moral theology will still be inadequately brought out unless an attempt is made also to exhaust as far as possible the *meaning* of the moral truths and to obtain a better idea of their true *value*.

Moral theology and casuistry

From what the Council Fathers say about the scientific character of moral theology and from their general references to that science (Training for the Priesthood 16), it is plain that they do not want a lop-sided casuistically-oriented moral theology. The virtues and duties characteristic of the Christian vocation should certainly not be determined and demonstrated from casuistic solutions to a whole series of questions, even granted that casuistry necessarily includes the application of moral principles. Much more important in this connection is the scientific working-out and appraisal of fundamental moral principles, which we have already discussed. Admittedly a moral theology that insists on the universal validity of moral principles and also considers how they should be applied in individual cases, is designated casuistic by most Protestant theologians. They defend their attitude by saying that a moral theology of this sort has a ready-made *a priori* solution for prospective, and even potential, situations: such a system they reject on grounds largely connected with their doctrine relating to man's condition after the Fall and his subsequent coming under the dominion of God's redeeming love. This accusation of Protestant theologians and also the discussions that have more recently arisen among Catholic theologians should certainly make us very cautious. Above all, we must examine as scrupulously as possible whether certain general principles formulated by us have, in fact, the scope of application indicated by their wording. It is *we*, of course, and not God, who put them into words, and our judgements and manner of expressing them can be very inexact indeed.

Ours is a moral theology of absolute principles and this being so there is no reason why we should reject the use of a balanced casuistry; by discussing 'moral cases', by taking them as patterns, so to speak, we may elucidate the true meaning of the basic principles involved. Moreover, casuistry can help us to discover the moral aspect and value of the various concrete data involved, and this applies whether the data are similar to the data of the case that has been solved or are completely unforeseen. The future priest's formation so far as moral theology is concerned would not be complete without an adequate knowledge of casuistry. And the moral theologian suffers no slight to his dignity by venturing into the more practical domain of casuistry; it is part of his task to do so. His casuistry should not, however, occupy itself with futile questions or be excessively concerned with calculations as to what constitutes the *minimum* needed to fulfil a Christian's obligations. And it certainly should never lose sight of the Christian's every-day duty to do justice to his high vocation in Christ.

To understand aright the relation of moral principles to casuistry it must first of all be borne in mind that 'case' (*casus*) and 'situation' are not the same thing. *Case* denotes a more or less concretely-presented, personal (i.e. involving a person or persons) combination of circumstances whose 'solution' is to be found in a universally valid judgement. This judgement of 'solution' holds good whenever the precise combination of circumstances in respect of which that judgement was formed, is again met with. *Situation*, on the contrary, denotes that absolutely unique, non-recurring personal combination of circumstances about which a moral judgement is formed in the conscience at the very moment that combination of circumstances takes place. It must also be noted that a situation cannot be resolved, quite simply, by a prefabricated judgement—be this taken from sacred Scripture or tradition or the Church's magisterium or arrived at by logical argument from a general principle or a case decided. It is rather that the conscience of the person involved—assuming it is a correct or true conscience—tells him the principles and indicates the solutions that apply here and now. His conscience, moreover, gives him insight into any moral elements of the situation which have not been completely resolved by those principles and solutions. The situation, for instance, may call for something more than the strict application of principles; its tenseness may make exceptional demands upon his spiritual resources.

From what we have said it ought now to be clear that the art of casuistry has a definite place in a scientific moral theology and also what the nature of its task should be. It must, on the one hand, recognize that the working-out and appraisal of fundamental principles always have priority, while, on the other hand, it will be charged with seeing that the principles and 'solutions' function properly in the formation of judgements of conscience in any particular situation.[14]

Moral theology and anthropology

The scientific treatment of moral theology necessitates the study of certain data of theological, philosophical and psychological anthropology. Free acceptance of our vocation in Christ and its fulfilment in practice cannot be adequately understood without a corresponding knowledge of the nature of man, to whom Christ's call is addressed, and of the way in which man's nature operates.

The first point that must be clarified before we can call

[14]For the value and the limitations of casuistry and for bibliography cf. E. Hamel, *Loi naturelle et loi du Christ*, Bruges 1964, 45–77.

our moral theology 'scientific' concerns the relation between the 'natural' and the 'supernatural' in man and, more especially, natural law and its place in the law of Christ which is our sole moral law.[15] Modern marriage problems have been mainly responsible for raising a question that has now become acute: How can man's nature and the natural law that corresponds with it be recognized or determined? But there is an even more important question, a fundamental one: How does natural law stand in relation to those elements of the law of Christ which, without being opposed to natural law are, nevertheless, not 'natural'? It must be made clear to students that the elements of natural law are, in fact, elements of a supernatural moral order, although they are not supernatural in the same way as those elements that are *inherently* supernatural and do not, therefore, belong to the natural order. It must be shown how the requirements of natural law can be fulfilled in a supernatural way and how faith, hope and that Christian love which we call charity, must inspire and pervade this fulfilment. It must be shown, too, how far natural law itself and its fulfilment are a means of supernatural salvation; or, more precisely, how they are a means which enable faith, hope and charity to express themselves, and how they are a means of salvation because of that and not merely because they are 'natural law and its fulfilment'. Lastly, there must be an examination of the reasons why the scientific treatment of natural law belongs to moral *theology* as theology, and the authoritative exposition of natural law belongs to the Church's *magisterium*; this is another matter that has recently become acute. All these points call for treatment commensurate with their importance and failing this it will be impossible to explain satisfactorily why and how our observance of natural law is, in fact, merely living up to our Christian vocation.

The second important question that requires discussion in depth during the course in moral theology concerns the

---

[15]See the relevant bibliography in **note 26.**

distinction between the primary and the secondary element of the New Law, the law of Christ, as elaborated in particular by St Thomas Aquinas from the writings of St Paul and St Augustine.[16] This distinction, taken from St Thomas's discussion of the problem 'Law and Gospel (Grace)' should on no account be allowed to fall into oblivion. Without it there would be an inadequate understanding of the reaction of the Christian vocation in a given situation. The written precepts of the gospel and the unwritten precepts of natural law are equally 'external' to sinful, 'carnal' man; to him they are law imposed from outside. But the grace of the holy Spirit is an 'interior' law for redeemed, 'spiritual' man; this is a law that enlightens, guides and animates him from within to such effect that he obeys not because he is compelled by an external force to do so but because he is compelled by the Spirit of love within him. This interior law is the primary element of the New Law, the law of Christ. It is not opposed to or inconsistent with the external demands which are the secondary element of the New Law; it interiorizes them, transforming the quality of their fulfilment by the power of faith and love. This interior law takes into account the moral necessities of the individual as such. It takes over, indeed, the entire moral guidance of the individual. The distinction between the primary and the secondary element of the New Law, therefore, involves something fundamentally different from that type of situational ethics which would question the validity of general laws in concrete situations. The distinction drawn by St Thomas enables us to get a better idea of how much even a genuinely

---

[16]On this distinction of St Thomas cf. *S. theol.* Ia IIae, q. 106–8; also T. A. Deman, *Der neue Bund und die Gnade,* Heidelberg 1955, 287–325. On law and gospel cf. A. Forster, *Evangelium und Gesetz bei Girolamo Seripando,* Paderborn 1965; B. Häring, 'Die Stellung des Gesetzes in der Moraltheologie', *Moralprobleme im Umbruch der Zeit* (ed. V. Redlich), Munich 1957, 133–52; S. Lyonnet, 'Liberté chrétienne et loi de l'Esprit selon St Paul', *Christus* (4) 1954, 6–27; G. Söhngen, *Gesetz und Evangelium,* Munich 1957 and his article 'Gesetz und Evangelium' in *Catholica* (14) 1960, 81–105; A. Valsecchi, 'Gesù Cristo nostra legge', *Scuola Cattolica* (88), 1960, 81–110, 161–90.

individualistic system, such as existential ethics or situational ethics (of the right type), can help us to perceive and understand the absolutely concrete vocation in Christ (that is, what Christ wants us to do) in a given situation. And a knowledge of the function of the Christian's conscience in such a situation can, of course, also contribute to the same end.

The third question that must be considered in connection with the scientific exposition of the Christian vocation concerns the personal character of the moral act. Opinion is unanimous that the moral act, which has been the subject of so much abstract speculation, is a moral act only in an analogous sense. The adjective 'moral', in the strict sense of the word, can only be applied to an act that proceeds authentically from the personality of whoever performs it. But a moral act is more than a specific, authentic act of a particular person. It is, at the same time, an attempt at self-realization on the part of the whole personality of whoever performs it—of the person, that is, in his personal and supernatural relation to God. To be sure, this self-realization takes place when the act is performed—in pre-conceptual consciousness. Indeed it is precisely on this account that the act acquires its moral quality (and its merit before God), because in and through that specific act the individual self (and its relation to God) is realized.

It can happen, nevertheless, that for one reason or another a specific act of a particular person in this process of self-realization is imbued with his personality only to a small extent or barely or not at all, possibly because the act, being performed in time and space, is governed by the psychical condition and efforts of the person who performs it. Hence the fundamental question arises as to the extent to which the doer's personality enters into a specific act of his. This is the reason why the degree of good or evil of a particular act is held to depend more on the extent to which the doer's personality is involved than on the concrete nature of the act itself. What is more, it makes no difference whether the act is 'grave' (important) or 'petty' (unimportant), whether it is good or evil. The only moral act that can be called 'grave' is essentially one that emanates from, and is imbued with, the doer's personality, which freely controls it; its execution implements his basic decision (be it a first decision or a renewal) with regard to his vocation in Christ, for his act brings with it either divine favour or divine condemnation. From all this, two findings emerge which are important in appraising man's moral attitudes. Firstly, the individual's basic decision with regard to his vocation in Christ can be, and is indeed, intensified if he has hitherto lived up to his Christian vocation. Secondly, the individual who has made his decision for or against his vocation in Christ is capable of acts that run counter to that decision but are, nevertheless, not imbued with his personality and are not attempts at self-realization; such acts are therefore termed 'petty' or unimportant acts and may be good or evil. They do not change the doer's basic decision but they do incline him to change it.[17]

Our fourth major point is only too plain. It is that a scientific exposition of moral theology must certainly include a sound introduction to the problems of individual and social psychology. This might be given by psychologists and not by moral theologians (save for very special reasons). An act that has its origin not so much in man's free choice as in other powers within him cannot, surely, be the free and authentic act of man striving to realize himself in relation to God.

Catholic and non-Catholic moral theology

The Council requires that clerical students shall be 'led to a more adequate understanding' of non-Catholic Churches and shall also be 'introduced to a knowledge of the other (i.e. non-Christian) religions which are more widely spread through individual areas' (Training for the Priesthood 16). From the scientific standpoint this implies that the moral

---

[17]On the 'basic decision' and its influence on the 'basic intention' cf. note 25.

theology course shall include an introduction to, and assessment of, the corresponding non-Catholic ethical systems, religious and profane. Comparison with other systems can lead to a better understanding of our own doctrine and a more rigorous scrutiny of the reasons behind our own position. At the same time other ethical systems must be explored with an eye to the elements in them that are true—and also to those they contain that are less coherent or plainly unsound.

Relation of moral theology to ethics and dogmatics

The scientific exposition of moral theology labours under not a few well-known difficulties arising from the fact that ethics and dogmatic theology, to both of which moral theology stands in special relation, are independent disciplines and are therefore taught apart from moral theology.

Philosophical ethics, both general and special, and in particular social ethics, are usually taught not only separately from, but at an earlier stage than, moral theology, in the seminary syllabus. This gives rise to the following difficulties.

Many questions that could also be discussed in philosophical ethics are usually reserved on practical grounds for moral theology. This practice can suggest to the student that there is a greater difference between philosophical ethics and moral theology than is theoretically justifiable. The danger in this is that it makes it hard for students to understand that ethics, although taught separately, has its own place in moral *theology*. A whole series of questions in general ethics and many questions in social ethics could just as well be dealt with in moral theology, which indeed already handles many other questions that are proper to 'rational' ethics. Many other questions, too, that admit of purely *rational* solutions are treated in the moral theology course. On the other hand, many questions ordinarily reserved for philosophical ethics have reference to revelation or Church doctrine. Whether it is decided ultimately to apportion the teaching of morality between a philosophical course and a theological one or whether it is thought better to keep it all within a single course, certain difficulties are sure to persist. Whichever solution is chosen it will be necessary to make clear to students the sense in which all moral truths concern man's response in his everyday life to his vocation in Christ.

Dogmatic and fundamental theology in *theory* should precede moral theology, which itself is best considered, for practical reasons, as a continuation of the former. But in fact moral theology is now usually taught before, or concurrently with, dogmatic theology. This creates difficulties that should not be underestimated for they are a real hindrance to the student in grasping the true and full significance of Christian morality. This is especially felt in the tracts on fundamental morality or the theological virtues or the sacraments. Can any completely satisfactory method be suggested for removing these obstacles?

Moral theology in the theological faculties

The Council requires that the scientific character of moral theology shall be impressed on *all* our future priests. Nevertheless it distinguishes different degrees of scientific method having in mind particularly the difference between seminary training and that given in theological faculties and in universities. Theology in the faculties and universities is to be taught in accordance with the 'higher scientific method' (Training for the Priesthood 18). Certain knotty questions especially 'should be left for higher academic studies' (*ibid.* 17). Suitable candidates should be sent to the faculties and universities in order to prepare them for the various needs of the apostolate (*ibid.* 18; Missions 26). These needs are set out more precisely in the Decree on Christian Education where they are described as 'teaching in seats of higher Church studies, advancing various branches of knowledge and undertaking the more arduous tasks of the intellectual apostolate' (Education 11). In the same Decree there is a detailed statement of what is expected from the theological faculties: 'It is the responsibility of the faculties to explore more profoundly the various areas of the sacred disciplines so that day by day a deeper understanding of sacred revelation will be developed, the treasure of Christian wisdom handed down by our ancestors will be more plainly brought to view, dialogue will be fostered with our separated brothers and with non-Christians, and solutions will be found for problems raised by the development of doctrine' (*ibid.*).

The theological faculties, then, are charged with promoting theology and the cognate sciences. To do so necessitates the use of 'more recent methods and teaching aids'; teachers are exhorted also to 'lead their listeners on to more searching inquiries' (*ibid.*). It stands to reason that the quality of scientific method in the seminaries and in the faculties varies appreciably not only according to the kind of previous training received by the professors and students but also according to the different external circumstances under which studies are carried out. There is no doubt, however, that the Council's remarks on the study of moral theology in the seminaries are also meant to apply to courses in the theological faculties.

V. HOW MORAL THEOLOGY IS TO BE RENEWED

The Council Fathers call for a renewal—or rather for the better development (*perficienda*)—of moral theology: the time has come at last for a change in the simple and uncomplicated approach to this subject which has prevailed (more or less) throughout a very long period indeed. The form this development is meant to take has been indicated in the passages from the Council documents which we have already discussed. If the Council's intentions are to be fulfilled, two points in particular have to be born in mind:

moral theology has never yet—strictly speaking—attained the ideal contemplated by the Council;

the Council's downright and unequivocal injunction cannot be entirely explained by a certain uneasiness on its part about the almost 'traditional' matter and method of moral theology: it shows rather that the Council is aware of significant trends in contemporary thinking on the subject.

An unrealized ideal

As a matter of fact no real tradition of the ideal moral theology contemplated by the Council exists today. Some elements of it are to be found occasionally in certain types of moral theology which have appeared at various times in history.

The moral message of holy Writ is certainly devoid of any attempt at system or scientific method. The early Christian writers strove hard to discern from the Scriptures what was the full content of the moral law that belonged to the saving mystery of Christ. In the writings of the period we can also see other views than theirs, views derived mainly from the relatively high quality of profane culture at the time. A few writings that show signs of scientific method began to appear; those of St Augustine in particular come to mind. The innumerable works with a moral content that have come down to us from the centuries which intervened between the Fathers of the Church and the Schoolmen—for example the various works 'On the Virtues and Vices' and the Penitentials —display neither scientific method nor active contact with the Christian mystery. Scholastic theology of the later Middle Ages included moral questions in its systematic exposition of Church doctrine. It often showed a grasp of scientific method that fell little short of perfection, but all too frequently it was not rooted in the saving mystery of Christ, at least in the form desired by the Council Fathers. Furthermore, it lacked that unity of a discipline influenced by, yet independent of, dogmatic theology—that very unity which is demanded by the moral theology of today. Medieval dissertations on mystical theology, like the Penitentials, were naturally one-sided. Sixteenth-century theology produced some excellent works on moral theory but much in them can hardly be called distinctively Christian. Since the seventeenth century the *Institutiones Morales* and the manuals that came after them form the bulk of the literature of moral theology. They contain much matter that is especially useful to confessors and spiritual directors. But they are often sadly lacking in that very quality which the Council now demands from moral theology, namely, that it shall be capable of demonstrating 'the nobility of the Christian vocation of the faithful'. And the scientific quality of this literature is uneven. There has come into use in Germany since the beginning of the nineteenth century a type of moral theology that lays more stress on contact with the saving mystery of Christ and on the nobility of the Christian vocation than any of the manuals just mentioned.[18]

Present trends

The ideal that the Council sets for moral theology has so far never been achieved in the history of that science. Nevertheless moral theologians have no need to begin all over again; at least they have something to go on. Some of the elements in the Council's ideal have already been evident in one or other of the various types of courses in that subject. During the last few decades, especially, several significant advances have been made towards the ideal.[19] We have already remarked that the Council's insistence on the development of moral theology was not entirely due to uneasiness about the inadequacy of the content and method of a familiar type of course. The primary reason for this insistence is that not a few theologians, even before the

[18]For tendencies that have arisen during the past century in Germany see J. Dieboldt, *La théologie morale catholique en Allemagne au temps du philosophisme et de la restauration* 1750–1850, Strasbourg 1926; and P. Hadrossek, *Die Bedeutung des Systemgedankens für die Moraltheologie in Deutschland seit der Thomas-Renaissance,* Munich 1950.

[19]Cf. E. Hirschbrich, *Die Entwicklung der Moraltheorie im deutschen Sprachgebiet seit der Jahrhundertwende,* Klosterneuburg 1959; and P. Delhaye, 'Die gegenwärtigen Bestrebungen der Moraltheologie in Frankreich', *Moralprobleme im Umbruch der Zeit* (ed. V. Redlich), Munich 1957, 13–39. Cf. also note 22 below.

Council had come together, were planning or had actually
carried out some revisions in the 'traditional' type of course
that were on the lines subsequently laid down by the Council.
It is very likely, too, that much more had already occurred
in the theological faculties than had found its way into print
by way of articles or text-books. But it cannot be denied that
the moral theology presented in Fritz Tillmann's *Die Idee der
Nachfolge Christi*[20] was a highly significant beginning, despite
a certain biblical bias. The same can be said of Bernhard
Häring's *Das Gesetz Christi*[21] which has had so much success
and influence, greater perhaps outside academic circles
than within them.

In the meantime a good many articles and books have
appeared in which the various elements required for a
renewal of moral theology have been discussed. The
suggestions put forward are, for the most part positive and
constructive; only rarely do we find a downright negative
attitude.[22] As a result there is a great deal of good work now

[20]F. Tillmann, *Handbuch der katholischen Sittenlehre*, III, Düsseldorf 1933
(4th edn. 1953).

[21]B. Häring, *The Law of Christ* (tr. E. G. Kaiser), Cork 1961–3.

[22]On the perfection of moral theology cf. P. Anciaux, 'Morale chrétienne et
monde contemporain', *Collectanea Mechlinensia*, (49) 1964, 323–42; *ibid.*,
'Dynamische perspectiven in de moraal', 343–63; *ibid.*, 'Religion et morale.
Les vraies perspectives de la morale chrétienne', 409–30; P. Anciaux and
A. D'Hoogh, *Pour un renouveau de la morale chrétienne*, Mechelen 1964; A. Auer,
'Anliegen heutiger Moraltheologie', *Theologische Quartalschrift*, (138) Tübingen
1958, 275–306; F. Böckle, 'Bestrebungen in der Moraltheologie', *Fragen der
Theologie heute* (ed. J. Feiner, J. Trütsch, F. Böckle), Einsiedeln 1957, 425–46;
Juan de Castro, 'Cristo el centro de nuestra vida moral', *Teología y Vida* (6)
1965, 115–27; F. Clark, 'The Challenge to Moral Theology', *Clergy Review*
(38) 1953, 214–23; W. Conway, 'The Science of Morals. New Trends', *Irish
Theological Quarterly* (22) 1955, 154–8; P. Delhaye, 'La théologie morale d'hier
et d'aujourd'hui', *Revue des Science Religieuses*, Strasbourg (27) 1953, 112–30;
G. Ermecke, 'Die katholische Moraltheologie heute. Ein Beitrag zu ihrer
Weiterentwicklung', *Theologie und Glaube* (41) 1951, 127–42; S. Festorazzi,
'Una recente morale del Nuovo Testamento e il problema del Nuovo Testa-
mento e il problema del metodo', *La Scuola Cattolica* (93) 1965, 217–21; G.
Ermecke, 'Die katholische Moraltheologie im Wandel der Gegenwart',
Theologie und Glaube 1963, 348–66; J. C. Ford, and G. Kelly, *Contemporary
Moral Theology* I, 60–103; L. B. Gillon, *Cristo e la Teologia Morale*, Rome 1961;

available on biblical themes, moral concepts and other biblical elements relating to moral theology.[23] There is no dearth of articles and papers on the theological aspect of moral questions; they are concerned mainly with the Christocentric character of morals in general; specific theological motifs for a more homogeneous presentation of moral theology; the problems of nature-and-grace and of

B. Häring, 'The Dynamism of Christian Life', *Chicago Studies* (4) 1965, 253–73; *id.*, 'Heutige Bestrebungen zur Vertiefung und Erneuerung der Moraltheologie', *Studia Moralia* (1), Rome 1963, 11–38; J. Hoefnagels, 'Erneuerung der Moral', *Wort und Wahrheit* (21) 1966; E. McDonagh, 'Moral Theology: The Need of Renewal', *Moral Theology Renewed* (ed. E. McDonagh), Dublin 1965; G. Thils, *Tendances actuelles en théologie morale*, Gembloux 1940; I. Zeiger, 'Katholische Moraltheologie heute', *Stimmen der Zeit* (68), Freiburg 1938, 143–53; *id.*, 'De condicione theologiae moralis moderna', *Periodica de re morali canonica liturgica* (28), Rome 1939, 177–89; J. G. Ziegler, 'Zur Gestalt und Gestaltung der Moraltheologie', *Trierer Theologische Zeitschrift* (71), Trier 1962, 46–55.

On the relation of moral theology to dogmatic theology cf. K. Rahner, 'Dogmatik', *Lexikon für Theologie und Kirche* III, 446 f.; *ibid.*, *Theological Investigations* I, (tr. C. Ernst), London 1961; P. Delhaye, 'Dogme et morale', *Analecta Gregoriana* (64), Rome 1954, 27–39; M. J. Vieujean, 'Dogmatique et morale', *Revue d'histoire ecclésiastique* (27), Lyon 1935–6, 333–8.

[23]Among the better-known studies are the following: C. H. Dodd, *Gospel and Law*, London 1951; R. Schnackenburg, *Moral Teaching of the New Testament* (tr. Holland-Smith and O'Hara), London 1964; C. Spicq, *Théologie morale du Nouveau Testament* (2 vols.), Paris 1965; also W. Crotty, 'Biblical Perspectives in Moral Theology', *Theological Studies* (26), Baltimore 1965, 574–96; J. Etienne, 'Théologie morale et renouveau biblique', *Ephemerides Theologicae Lovanienses* (40), Bruges 1964, 232–41; G. Friedrich, 'Christus, Einheit und Norm des Christen. Das Grundmotive des 1. Korintherbriefs', *Kerygma und Dogma* (9) 1963, 235–58; A. Humbert, 'L'observance des commandements dans les écrits johanniques', *Studia moralia* I, Rome 1963, 187–219; J. Jeremias, *The Central Message of the New Testament*, London 1965; E. Neuhäusler, *Anspruch und Antwort Gottes*, Düsseldorf 1962; N. Lazure, *Les Valeurs morales de la théologie johannique*, Paris 1965; W. Pfister, *Das Leben im Gebot nach Paulus*, Freiburg 1963; Thüsing, *Per Christum in Deum: Studien zum Verhältnis von Christozentrik und Theozentrik in den paulinischen Hauptbriefen*, Münster 1965. For particular themes, e.g., Law, see J. M. Aubert, *Loi de Dieu, loi des hommes*, Paris 1965; Conscience, see P. Delhaye, *La conscience morale du chrétien*, Paris 1964, 17–48; Sin, see A. Gelin, 'Le péché dans l'Ancient Testament', *Théologie du Péché* I, Paris 1960, 23–49; A. Descamps, 'Le péché dans le Nouveau Testament', *ibid.* 49–125; S. Lyonnet, 'Péché', *Suppl. Dictionnaire Biblique VII*, Paris 1964, 481–567; Justice, see E. Hamel, 'L'usage de l'Écriture Sainte en théologie morale', *Gregorianum* (47) 1966, 77–84. For other themes see *Das Theologische Wörterbuch zum Neuen Testament* (ed. E. Kittel), Stuttgart.

natural moral law seen from the standpoint of moral theology; and the question of a suitable methodology for the exposition of moral theology.[24] Numerous articles have appeared on theological, philosophical and psychological anthropology; these contribute substantially to the better understanding of what is meant by a (supernatural) moral life. They develop such ideas as the mediation of a specific moral element—of faith or charity, for instance—by a particular moral act; the idea of non-reflexive, pre-conceptual consciousness; the basic decision and the basic intention that flows from it; the analogous nature of moral categories—of, for example, the 'grave' (or important) and the 'petty' (or unimportant) moral act.[25] Much has been

[24]A very full bibliography of theological motifs will be found in R. Hofmann, *Moraltheologische Erkenntnis- und Methodenlehre*, Munich 1963, 11–22, 217–52. On the nature-and-grace problem see J. Arntz, 'Natural Law and its History', *Concilium* (1) 1965, 23–31; P. Delhaye, *Permanence du droit naturel* (Anal. Med. Namur, 10), Lyon n.d.; K. Demmer, *Ius caritatis: Zur christologischen Grundlegung der augustinischen Naturrechtslehre* (Analecta Gregoriana, vol. 118), Rome 1961; J. Fuchs, *Natural Law* (tr. Reckter and Dowling), Dublin 1965; *id.*, *Theologia moralis generalis* I, Rome 1963; 21–110; B. Schüller, *Die Herrschaft Christi und das weltliche Recht*, Rome 1963; *id.*, 'Wie weit kann die Moraltheologie das Naturrecht entbehren?', *Lebendiges Zeugnis* 1965, 41–65. On methodology cf. R. Hofmann *op. cit.*; W. A. Wallace, 'The Role of Demonstration in Moral Theology', *Texts and Studies* II, Washington 1962.

[25]On mediation cf. the works of G. Gilleman and K. Rahner quoted in note 5 above. On the basic decision see M. Flick-Z. Alszeghy, 'L'opzione fondamentale della vita morale e la grazia', *Gregorianum* (41) 1960, 593–619; C. V. Truhlar, *Structura theologica vitae spiritualis*, Rome 1958; P. Fransen, 'Pour une psychologie de la grace divine', *Lumen vitae* (12) 1957, 209–40; J. Maritain, *Raison et raisons*, Paris 1947, 131–65; *id.*, *Neuf leçons sur les notions premières de la philosophie morale*, Paris 1949, 119–28; J. B. Metz, 'Befindlichkeit', *Lexikon für Theologie und Kirche* II, Freiburg 1958, 102–4; S. Dianich, 'La corruzione della natura e la grazia nelle opzioni fondamentali', *Scuola Cattolica* (92) 1964, 203–20. On the action of the basic decision on the moral life through the medium of the basic intention, see H. Reiners, 'Grundintention und sittliches Tun', *Quaestiones disputatae* 30, Freiburg 1966. For the analogy between mortal and venial sin on the one side and great and little good on the other cf. J. B. Metz, 'Zur kategorialen Differenzierung des Freiheitsvollzuges', *Gott in Welt I*, Freiburg 1964, 312–414: B. Schüller, 'Zur Analogie sittlicher Grundbegriffe', *Theologie und Philosophie* (41) 1966, 3–19: P. Schoonenberg, 'Zonde ten dode, doodzonde en dagelijkse zonde', *Tijdschrift voor Theologie* (3) 1961, 181–93; K. Rahner, *Theological Investigations* I (tr. C. Ernst), London 1961, 347 f.; *ibid.*, III (tr. K. H. and B. Kruger), London 1967, 154 f.

written on moral psychology, and phenomenological studies
have made no small contribution to the development of
moral theology.[26] Historical studies now available on specific
questions, or particular periods, of moral theology are of the
utmost importance for the right understanding and teaching
of the subject itself. Moreover, there has been much pains-
taking investigation into the theological and philosophical
aspects of general principles and particular problems,
especially those that have recently become burning questions.
As examples we might point to the many questions of social
morality that have been dealt with over the last few years,
and to the fact that the Council Fathers did not deliver their
declaration on religious freedom without recourse to the
fruitful labours of the theologians. And lastly we must not
omit to mention the difficult marriage problems for which so
many theologians have striven so hard to work out a
solution.

The factors so briefly set out here moved the Council
Fathers to exhort theologians to renew the presentation of
Christian moral teaching. The same factors can now help
theologians to comply—though as yet only imperfectly—with
the Council's demand for a more scientific exposition of
moral theology that will really pave the way for understanding the nobility of the Christian vocation of the faithful.

[26]See the works of M. Scheler and D. von Hildebrand's *Christliche Ethik*,
Düsseldorf 1959 with commentary thereon of R. Egenter in *Salzburger Jahrbuch
für Philosophie* (5–6) 1961–2, 351–63.

2 The Christian Morality of Vatican II[1]

In keeping with the Second Vatican Council, Christian morality could become the topic of many very different lectures. If you work your way through the thoughts treated in the Dogmatic Constitution on the Church, thoughts that are authentically Christian and rooted in the spirit of holy Scripture, you will be gripped by the Church's conviction that the whole Christian People of God of the Church and all its members are called to the fullness of Christian perfection and holiness. The Pastoral Constitution on the Church in the Modern World testifies before all the world how much the Church is interested in the morally correct accomplishment of the many tasks which the world's realities give the Christian. In the Decree on the Training of Future Priests, the Council gives a brief, pithy direction for the teaching of moral theology in seminaries. There it says that before all else this teaching must set forth the exalted vocation to which Christ calls the faithful and the consequences flowing from that call.

So the Council deals with many factors of Christian morality. The following very characteristic factors must be singled out: (I) Christian morality is a morality of a call-in-Christ; (II) Christian morality is a morality of the Church; (III) Christian morality is a morality for the world today.

---

[1]One of a series of lectures given by European theologians on the theology of the Second Vatican Council to the Loyola Academy in Willmette (Chicago), May, 1967.

I. A MORALITY OF THE CALL IN THE PERSON OF
CHRIST

Christ as the foundation of Christian morality

The Council believed that before all else it should remind
Christians of the fact that their morality is based on the
person of Christ who came into this world. It may sound
strange to many people, perhaps to many Christians and
Catholics, that in reality, and not only as some seemingly
pious thought, their day-by-day morals and the morality of
the whole of life, should be centred in Christ. This one person,
Christ, should determine the morals of all our living, beginning with the external organization of the world in this
age of atomic power and nascent conquest of space, and all
the way down into our innermost personal thought and will
life. The Council is the protagonist of this 'madness', as
some call it, this faith, as we Christians see it, challenging the
whole man, a faith that we Christians draw from Christ and
by which we impart meaning to the world as a whole and
particularly to man's conduct. With the Council we
Christians dare to take this stand before the whole world of
the second half of the twentieth century.

In all this the Council is thinking, in the first instance, not
of the commandments and the demands of Jesus the lawgiver and preacher of morality, no matter how lofty and
idealistic—some would say utopian!—this may be. Nor is
the Council thinking of the moral preaching of Paul the
apostle, of what Paul so often directs 'in the Lord', 'in his
Name', to the Christian community. That was what many
Christian theologians and philosophers of the Enlightenment
were primarily concerned with. Not so the Second Vatican
Council.

The Council looks much more at the proper foundation
of Christian morality in the sublime call which has become
our portion in the person of Christ. This call is not only a
salutary warning to keep mindful of our dutiful existence
before the Creator-God. The Christian vocation means

E

rather the redemptive emancipation from the inner bond
binding people to a world fallen under the dominion of sin,
emancipation for salvation in him, the Son of God the
Father become Man. For that salvation is here at hand,
even today although it belongs to the future for its complete
fulfilment. Accordingly, the vocation of the Christian is
before all else gift and grace, but at the same time, *challenge*
and *command*—a challenge and command to live as one
redeemed—liberated (and not as bound to a world fallen
under the dominion of sin) and to live as one called to
salvation in Christ (and not as one abandoned to perdition).
Now seen in this light, this challenge-command, to live as
the free, the chosen, is in its inmost depth of reality a great
grace, namely, the grace-bearing summons to yield ourselves up and be redeemed, to have salvation bestowed upon
us, and, accordingly, to walk in the paths of those who accept
redemption and salvation in Christ. With the Council we
Christians think that those who have grasped by faith that
the Father in sending Christ has sent us and the whole world
the Saviour and Redeemer—such people will understand the
whole world in the light of Christ, and live their lives accordingly. With the Council, moreover, we Christians think like
this about our liberation and our salvation-call in Christ: it
is not only a possibility negotiable from without, a call from
beyond us. No, it transforms the Christian person from
within, full of grace to make us over for thinking and loving
the way Christ did. Consequently, our liberation, our calling
has made us (other) Christs just because it has fashioned us
anew by his favour. It is clearly bound to bear fruit in our
Christian living. The Christian call, freely welcomed, is so
powerful in us that our whole life is determined by it, from
our innermost thought and love to the shaping of our
world-view.

That is why we think as we do—yes, with the Council—
however utopian a ring it may have for our non-Christian
fellowmen. We think that the life of those who have been
called by Christ, in the measure that they accept his call,

will be made over into a life in the image of Christ, and even made into him who calls us. This is what we mean exactly: the life of those called in Christ, to the extent that they *are* Christians, will show forth the image of Christ. No one should offer objections like the following. Christ did not marry. He did not have twentieth-century marriage problems. He did not reside in big-city slum environments, nor in high society. He did not have to answer for possession of wealth in a prosperous economy, for an organized, technical society face to face with the widespread hunger of the world's poor. He did not know the great possibilities of a world atom-fed and atom-fearing. How could *he* possibly be the prototype and pattern of Christians in our century? How can we expect that the lives of Christians of our own times should exhibit the features of this other-age Jesus? Now it is true that he was an individual human being, lived in the conditions of his times, in the particular circumstances of his human situation, above all else, in the circumstances of his distinctive life-work as world Redeemer. But, as the Church Fathers were teaching as early as the first centuries of our Christian era, the Son of God came to make his own all humanity, including the particular characteristics of every individual human being. And so, if he, in the compass of our experience, lives only his own individual life, as the Son of God who assumes all human existence, does he not sustain in himself everything else, everybody else? And does not every man, in his own way, by his Christian life, show forth and, so to say, unfold Christ who incorporates each Christian into himself? Or are we not prepared to take seriously the word of the Apostle of the Gentiles that everything and everybody subsists in him, the Son of God, Jesus Christ? Isn't it true, then, that all human possibilities and situations —those of our century, those of today—are grounded in him? So that the correct mastery of them in this or that person is a realization, a substantialization, an actuation, of Christ in our time? So it is actually he, 'the firstborn of all creation', who is the original which has to be reflected again and again in varying ways. In all this we must bear in mind too that such reflection, such 'imaging' of Christ is to be done by people belonging to a world invaded by sin, people who themselves experience the insistent downward pull of sin, but who nonetheless believe that they possess as their own the conquering strength of Christ. For that Christ whom each of us, in his own way, must actualize in the world is not only 'the firstborn of all creation'. He is also 'the firstborn from the dead'. This means that we Christians are created in him, but also recreated and freed from the power of sin by reason of his death and resurrection. We must, then, express in our lives the features, the spirit, of the God-man Jesus Christ.

The central meaning of the Spirit of Christ in us

I do not know if there was ever a Council that emphasized as strongly the presence in us of the tirelessly active holy Spirit, the Spirit of Christ, as did the Second Vatican Council in its various documents, thus keeping faith with the letter and the spirit of holy Scripture. The holy Spirit in us, the Spirit of Jesus Christ, wishes just this one thing: that we actuate our lives here and now in the manner and spirit of Christ. For this purpose before all else he makes us believe and hope and love. He brings about in us the commitment to God and to salvation in Christ which is the foundation of all Christian morality. Then he awakens in us the readiness and power to form the image of Christ in the many separate external expressions of our life. But he is also the Light that helps us to understand how behaviour in the Spirit of Christ must look in each and every situation. Certainly, we have the moral preaching of Christ and of St Paul. We have examples from our Lord's life. We have the moral directions of Christ's Church (whose very soul is the same holy Spirit). We have our own intellect, too, for understanding what given human situations demand of us morally. The holy Spirit, however, Christ's Spirit, is at work in us, to aid us in using rightly these various helps, for discovering genuine morality, and for guiding our concrete conduct to actually express the likeness to Christ which we are called to exhibit. Because of our human weakness we shall doubtless fail the truth often and in some individual questions, in spite of the light and urging of the holy Spirit. But on the whole, the Christian who does not shut out the working of the Spirit will be led to a life in the image of Christ. He will be led not only to faith and hope and love, but also to an organization and formation of his life and world that is more harmonious with Christ in every detail.

Now that we are speaking of the operation of the holy Spirit in us, we must mention above all what the Spirit first seeks to actuate in us, namely, faith grown into love. Love growing out of faith is Christian life in the most proper sense. Love in the manner of Christ loving the Father is essentially different from all other good works and virtues. In other virtues and good works, a person gives this or that. He always gives something; for example, in justice, obedience, magnanimity, chastity. In love, however, he does not dispose of this or that, but gives himself completely. He bestows himself as a person. So, what the Spirit of Christ wishes to effect in us above all is that we surrender to the Father not only this or that, but our heart, our entire selves, as Christ did. Everything else, the many tangible actions of every day, are—as a happy modern phrase has it (Gilleman) —mediations, that is ways and means for expressing our love as self-surrender to God. Total surrender to God can press every single moral act into its service as a means of self-development. It does not matter whether the moral act is an explicit expression of love of God, or any other act of our life. For, in every good moral act, we seek to produce not only this or that good, but we seek also and chiefly to express ourselves with greater actuality. We seek to express our whole selves as persons, self-yielding, self-surrendering to God; that is to say, we seek to love. The Christian living in grace does more in all his moral activity than each single reflexively conscious act indicates. He loves. He gives not only the good of that single act, but himself. This love of self-surrender fulfils itself, it is true, at a much deeper level in the soul than the particular moral act through which it manifests itself. The moral act, as the realization of a particular good, is completed on a level of the soul where we can extensively survey it in a reflexive way and as a particular object. But love, on the contrary, our own disposing of ourselves for self-surrender, is completed in that centre of the soul where we are, indeed, thoroughly aware of ourselves and our personal fulfilment and thoroughly conscious of our love without being able to identify and grasp it reflexively as a particular object. (This is that centre of the ego in which, in our opinion, even the agnostic and professed atheist in their individual acts come to morally responsible decisions about themselves as integral persons. Moreover these decisions are made before the Absolute which is God. For unless God is perceived, the absolute character of morality itself cannot be experienced. The agnostic and atheist are able to perceive God thus in the depths of the self, because there is question here, not of perceiving him as a person reflexively thought of, but of being non-reflexively conscious of him as a 'horizon', a Presence, before which alone can any activity be morally meaningful.) It is chiefly in this personal centre of the human soul that the holy Spirit endeavours to shape us into Christ. It is here, therefore, that we accept this working of the holy Sprit consciously, though not with reflexive awareness. This is true especially of those acts in which we are so personally involved that there is a genuine self-disposition. But it is also true of the everyday and rather 'superficial' acts. Even these acts the Spirit working in us seeks to orientate toward our total commitment. Through them the just man is to do good and thus make his love a little more visible; through them, too, the sinner is to do good and thus give evidence of the possibility and the beginning of his conversion.

Love—as the total self-disposition for God—is often designated by the Council as perfection. The Council devoted a special chapter to the call of all Christians to perfection. The holy Spirit takes hold of every believer and seeks to produce in him the life of Christ, namely, love. The Spirit of Christ in us and his work, love, do not recognize any self-complacency with separate good works, any contented standing-still. Abstinence on Friday and Sunday observance do not make a complete Christian. And whether it falls into our laps or is won in fierce combat, neither does our staying out of sins against truthfulness, justice, and chastity make us complete Christians; nor even freedom from all those sins that are catalogued in the examinations of conscience found in prayer books. All that belongs to being a Christian, but being a Christian forbids us to be satisfied with this. Love, according to the example of Christ and the Spirit producing it in us, presses us for more. It demands that we make the most of our talents, that we make proper use of the possibilities for well-doing, that we understand the quiet cry of our neighbour and of the world for understanding, love and help. It urges us, too, this love and the Spirit causing it, to grow in goodness, to begin anew after failures, and when we fear a failure to sincerely exert ourselves, and, finally, whatever goodness we think we have, to try to progress from good to better. The Council in speaking of the vocation of all believers to perfection, actually thinks that those who let themselves be seized by Christ increase continually and uninterruptedly in the likeness of the person of Christ. Christian morality, then, does not mean only fidelity to the catalogue of the commandments, but the uncataloguable, dynamic liveliness of the good, Spirit-inspired man, who detects opportunities for good with a fine sense and, above all, who does not deal so much in the 'thou shalt' of the commandments, but acts under the impulse of the 'thou mayest' of love.

Man and human morality in the morality of Christ

In the picture of Christian morality which the Council outlines we do not have to fear a lifeless, inhuman, other-worldly supernaturalism, of course. It is true that salvation is to be found only in grace and in the love it produces; but it is also true that what is at stake is the salvation of man, the gift of grace and love to man. How could the Council, which understands Christ the God-man as the prototype of Christian morality, have forgotten man? Just by pointing to Christ, the Council points to *that* Man, in whom according to St Paul, all that is human subsists. The endeavour of the Council tends to this: to bring man-in-Christ to man's fulfilment.

I am thinking here of a special problem, one which has been earnestly discussed again in recent years, namely, the meaning of the natural moral law in reference to Christ's morality. It would be inhuman, and a supernaturalism foreign to this world, to wish to separate the morality of natural law from Christian morality. Instead of denying or even depreciating the impact of natural law morality, or of the 'order of creation', as it is also called, the Council has repeatedly referred to this reality as God's ordaining. Especially by grounding Christian morality in the God-man, it reaffirmed natural law morality as the morality of man as man. Thus Christian morality also contains that morality grounded in man as such—natural law morality. Please let us not forget: we would not even understand the message of Christ's revelation about human realities and values like marriage, family, society, the state; like honesty, justice, selfless helpfulness—if we did not have a natural access to these realities and values, an understanding based on natural law. I am thinking especially about a sufficient and unerring knowledge of it. But does not our human interpretation of divine revelation also always run the danger of being inaccurate or even erroneous? In our understanding of both natural law morality and the morality of Christian revelation, we equally need the support of the holy Spirit, in individual people and the Church as a whole, to find the true picture of Christian morality, its unfalsified and adequate image.

Christian morality owes homage to no abstract super-naturalism which is foreign to the world, a supernaturalism that would forget man and his morality, namely, natural law morality. But neither does Christian morality pay homage to any naturalism separated from Christ. Man is, as a matter of fact, always man, created in Christ and called to salvation. Natural law morality is ordered to the redeeming Christ and his grace. Even the most faithful fulfilment of natural law morality (which we cannot actually achieve without Christ's grace) would not be able to make man just in the theological sense of the term. No deed complying only with the natural law, and no natural virtue, however elevated, could serve man unto salvation. Only in so far as such deeds and virtues are born and fulfilled by the love of Christ blooming out of faith—the love which the holy Spirit produces in us—are they, in a full sense, Christian deeds. Only then do they express the surrender of a human person to God in a Christlike manner. But faith and love will always do more than can ever be grasped on natural law grounds.

II. A MORALITY OF THE COMMUNITY OF THE CHURCH

A 'Church' morality

Now, it would be wrong to interpret the Christian morality we have just sketched as purely individualistic, a morality, namely, of each single man, who, called as an individual into Christ, tries to bring Christ's image to realization in his own life. This purely individualistic view is wrong from the start; for the message of reconciliation through Christ, and the message of the calling in Christ are found only in the Church, as the People of God. Only on the strength of the Church's preaching of the reconciliation and calling into Christ, do the faithful come to base the formation and organization of their life and world on the person of Christ.

On this point the Council leaves no room for doubt in the Dogmatic Constitution on the Church. We could add another observation here, too. The powerful grace-bearing sacramental signs, by which we become one with the Church and so, too, with Christ, are also the sacraments of the Church. Sacramental incorporation into the Church brings about a sacramental transformation into Christ. Christian morality is the morality of men who have been admitted into the People of God of the Church and who have thereby, too, become formed in Christ's image. Concerning this, too, the Council leaves no room for doubt.

Now, of course, the question arises: do we have to call Christian morality a Church morality? The foregoing explanations demand 'Yes' as an answer to this question. 'Yes' is demanded, too, in the sense that the moral message of Christ's revelation is found in the Church. This message is officially guarded and preached in the Church. Finally, the moral doctrine preached in the Church substantially expresses the morality of man sacramentally transformed into Christ.

But this truth about Christian morality being a 'Church morality' has another sense too. Aware of their calling in Christ and interiorly ready to let the person of Christ be the foremost model of their moral conduct, and willing, accordingly, to follow the compulsion of Christ's Spirit within them, the faithful simultaneously form an 'objective spirit', a 'Church awareness', a 'public concept' of Christian morality. This awareness of Christian morality within the Church emphasizes above all other values the basic value of the human person's offering of himself in faith, hope, and love. Do we doubt that this conviction can be found among the People of God in the Church? Moreover, the Church's moral awareness can distinguish numerous particular, separate values from specious values and utter absence of values. We do not infer that there are no open moral questions in the Church. These will always exist as long as God's People are a people made up of human beings. On the other hand,

not everything in the realm of morality is open to question
in the Church. Besides, it would be false to confuse an
individual's moral doubts with a general uncertainty within
the whole Church community. Certainly, the moral awareness of the Christian People of God is never perfect. It meets
several obstacles. First, there is the human weakness of the
men who constitute the People of God, and, secondly, the
faltering readiness to draw proper moral conclusions from
the vocation in Christ and to be sensitive to the demanding
and urging holy Spirit. But, nevertheless, the moral awareness founded on the person of Christ among the People of
God will remain substantially vital. Our guarantee is not
man, but the Spirit of Christ himself, who operates in each
one of the faithful and assists the Church as a whole, so that
her life might be the life of the First-Born of all men and of
all Christians, successfully imitated in substance, and thus
made visible.

*The presence of the Christian Church morality in the non-Christian
world*

We are confronted by the still important fact that the
explicit attempt is undertaken in this world in keeping with
man's call in Christ to let human life and human morality
be centred on the person of Christ. This is important for two
reasons: first, the morality centred on Christ who is for all
men the First-Born of all creation and of the dead is present
in this world. And this morality is not only present as a
private affair of many individuals, but as the awareness of
the Church's People of God. Secondly, this conscious
morality is visible beyond the boundaries of God's People.
The morality based on Christ teaches an unselfish disposition
of self as a whole. It wants fidelity to the words and example
of the Lord, to the regulation of the natural moral law and
to the directions of the Church. Christ-centred morality
condemns a complacent observance of the catalogued
commandments as insufficient and demands suitable action
in every situation and steady growth. This morality is

openly represented in the world and lived—although still deficiently—by a large yet relatively small group, namely, the members of the Church's People of God. And it is lived not only in private life, but also—we hope, at least—in the larger events of the world. The presence and visibility of the morality centred on the person of Christ are not adequately demonstrated therefore by the activity of the hierarchy and the priesthood. (These are only the ministry and the leaven.) They definitely demand the Christian life and Christian vitality of the many, who comprise the Church's People of God.

The morality of the non-Christian

The presence and visibility of the Christian-Church morality in the numerically greater non-Christian world brings up the question of non-Christian morality and its relationship to Christian morality. Are there really two different moralities, Christian and non-Christian, whereby one might be inclined to differentiate the non-Christian as based purely on the natural law? Or, is it not more correct to say with St Paul, that all of humanity is created in Christ and lives within the sphere of salvation because of his resurrection? From Paul's words it follows that there is really only one morality for everyone, namely, the morality founded on the person of Christ. The Christians, however, have stepped personally, sacramentally, and ecclesiastically into an explicit relationship with Christ. They can, with explicit awareness, allow Christ to become the form of their human life. Such explicit awareness of a Christian form of life is impossible for a non-Christian. But if all mankind, as created and redeemed, is already grounded in Christ, should we not say that in so far as the morality of a non-Christian is not false, but true and pure, it may have a part in the morality of Christians and so have its foundation in the person of Christ, instead of simply saying that it is in accord with the natural law? If this can rightly be said, however, then we must add that the morality of a non-Christian, in so far as it is pure and in accord with the moral natural law, stands in a relationship to Christ as the First-Born from the dead, which means to the Christ of salvation, grace, and Church. From this standpoint, the pure and good morality of a non-Christian is objectively (even if not with the complete awareness of the Christian) first, a true partnership already in the realization of the Christian and Church morality; and, secondly, always found in the service of grace and of the kingdom of Christ. Yes, in the service of the kingdom of Christ too. For two facts hold good for the natural law-based morality of the non-Christian, as for natural law morality in general. First, the good that belongs to it is destined, in the Christian order, to give the kingdom of Christ a chance for expansion. Who will deny that justice, benevolence, good education, responsible leadership in the state, and the like, on the part of non-Christians could serve as fertile soil for an eventual Christianity better than the opposite of these qualities? Secondly, what is true and good in the morality of non-Christians is destined in the Christian order to be fulfilled in faith and charity. Is not the genuine morality of non-Christians very often animated and filled with such believing love—Christian love? Not with the same explicit awareness, indeed, as for those who confess the name of Christ; rather it lies at the innermost depths of the soul which escape reflexive awareness. We said before that not only the non-Christian, but also the agnostic and the atheist make decisions about themselves in a non-reflexive awareness before the God of life. Neither can we exclude the possibility that they come to experience in this same non-reflexive way the grace of Christ urging them to a commitment of faith and love. (Christ offers himself, after all, to every human being.) If they do not reject this grace, they accept it. The Council itself reckons explicitly—and not only in one place—with this possibility. But if this is so, then such non-Christians are open to faith in their innermost souls, and their correct moral behaviour is an expression and 'mediation' of the love which Christ causes in them.

.In this regard, we must call the morality of Christians the explicit and Church-societal form of this morality, which non-Christians, too, realize in an implicit manner, possibly even mixed with many errors and with an explicit, but less deep, opposition to Christ and his Church. The Christians are those who, in an explicit manner and in a Church-community, direct the moral formation and organization of their life and world towards the person of Christ. They are a sign and help to those who do it in an incomplete and implicit, non-reflexive manner, and without the help of an explicit faith and the Church-community. The visibility of the morality founded on Christ's person has just this task: to help the non-Christian to a more explicit comprehension of not only the single elements, but also the deepest sense of the morality founded in Christ, which fundamentally constitutes their own morality.

III. A MORALITY FOR THE PRESENT WORLD

A 'realistic' morality

It has become obvious already that the Christian morality of the Council does not want to be just a morality of the personal private relationship of the individual with Christ, or just an inner Church morality without regard for the world. Christian morality does not mean a personal morality of solely formal abstract uprightness. Nor does it mean the morality of a closed ghetto. On the contrary, the Pastoral Constitution of the Council on the Church in the Modern World shows that a right viewpoint in the world and proper mastery of the world, even the world of today, matters very much to Christian morality. It is almost strange that we have to tell ourselves this in particular, for the man of Christian morality lives only in this world and is busy with its mastery.

What does the word 'world' mean? World is in its most essential sense man himself, or humanity, in any case, with all that belongs to it. That means, above all, human relations but also all the realities and possibilities of earth and space. So, the formation and organization of the world certainly signifies a creation of culture and of human relations, as well as the exploration and right exploitation of the earth and the whole universe. Viewed at a deeper level, however, the formation and organization of the world is concerned more than anything else with the formation and structure of man in the whole of the reality which is related to him.

This Christian world orientation has its own problematic. We know this world first as the creation coming from the hand of God. Secondly, we experience it, especially in man, as signed by the world, sin and its consequences. Thirdly, we believe in its salvation and its transcendent, grace-endowed, and eschatological calling and meaningfulness. Once again, we are speaking mainly of man, but also of the whole reality related to man—of human orders and institutions, and even of all events and possibilities beneath man. The Christian living in the world should try, first of all, to probe, evaluate, and master the inner meaning of the whole reality of creation. This whole reality would include the personal existence of man, human society and its various social forms, culture, politics, technology, and so forth. Secondly, in spite of the grace of salvation, he should take man's corruptibility seriously, since it could lead to egotistical autonomy instead of sensible mastery, for example, in the carrying out of technical, economic, or political possibilities. Thirdly, he should observe and always keep before his eyes the relativity of all worldly reality in comparison with its grace-endowed and eschatological transcendence. This moral attitude founded in Christ and taught by the Church can lead the individual believer to an emphatic withdrawal from the world, not out of anxiety or weakness, but to express the grace-filled, transcendent meaningfulness and calling of the world. Normally, it will lead a man to accept the world positively and form it according to the meaning of its creation and transcendent calling. Many do this in a manner consonant with their simple status in life with true humanity and

Christlikeness, but without any special problems. Others do it as a very reflexive and courageous self determination to exhaust the possibilities of the world grounded in Christ—in science, technology, politics, organization, social activity, use of economic and political power, and so forth.

A concrete morality

The 'world-nearness' of Christian morality implies its 'concreteness'. In a completely different way from that of the past, we experience the changeability of the world in our times. Not only does science, technology and experience present us with new questions. We see the changeability of man much more, too; for example, in his value judgements (he values much more today, for example, the personality of others—of all others—or he evaluates the social position of woman very differently than did a man of 300 or 600 years ago). The more deeply convinced the Christian is of the grounding in the person of Christ of morality in general and of the correct moral behaviour for each concrete single case, the more he will be concerned to reflect on the correct handling of his life situation. What went by the name of a *nouvelle Morale* or a certain *Situationsethik* in post-war middle Europe, and what is now appearing in Anglo-Saxon countries as a 'new morality', is not totally in error. It contains some valuable insights too. For it demands that we take the whole concrete reality seriously, especially the 'thou' of the other person and the demands resulting from our confrontation with him. It forbids a simple, matter-of-fact, cold 'imposition' of prefabricated principles on living reality. Obviously, the Christian morality of the Council does not agree with the relativizing of the moral absoluteness of true moral principles often implied in all this. Yet on the other hand, Christian morality too demands, not that we solve the problems which confront us coolly and impersonally by merely hauling out pre-printed principles, but that we should look at the complete concrete reality in all its living pro- portions and Christian humanness. In doing this we may have to inquire whether or not certain principles known to us already fit precisely this reality (ready to apply them, if they do). For example, the Council did not take lightly the question as to whether and how the familiar principles about a just war are still adequate for the reality which a modern total war would be. Possibly certain moral principles are formulated only for very definite conditions which, however, were not expressed in the original formulation, since in other times men could not even imagine different situations. Moreover, it would be rash to believe that humanly formulated principles are always absolutely correct and exact. Did not Pope Paul VI face such an eventuality when he submitted certain marriage questions to a study commission in 1964, in order to tell the world, in case an error should appear—though surely he himself hardly believed it would? Finally, there are always completely new questions which never appeared as such in former times and now demand a solution. We might point out an example in connection with the unfolding possibilities of modern biology for far-reaching arbitrary control of the future of the human species. In such a case it will often not be sufficient just to open up an old morals book. One will have to work much more with the concrete case itself to discover how a genuinely human and Christian handling of the new situation should look—human and Christian, I mean, in keeping with the image of Christ the God-man. For some questions, perhaps, it will be impossible to find immediately an exact solution, especially when a clear answer supposes scientific knowledge about the eventual consequences of certain solutions. In such a case there remains, for Christian morality too, only the duty of courageous and prudent decision within the realm of the given possibilities—and not without the risk of error.

Social responsibility

The Christian explicitly knows that truth and morality of the world-structure are founded on the person of Christ. He is not limited simply to his own deliberations about the

F

content he finds there. Consequently, he will consider himself in some degree co-responsible for other thinkers', even non-Christian thinkers', correctly envisaging that world-structure. The acceptance of this social responsibility belongs to his moral duty in and for this world. His serious reflection together with others—while he remains constantly aware of his calling in Christ—and the obviousness of his own life and activity in this world are of the highest importance here. How often the Council spoke of the importance of the Christian laity in this regard! And should we not speak of responsibility too, where the individual Christian shapes his whole seemingly personal and private life, in his inner make-up, where he permits inclinations and tendencies to arise and grow in his soul? For even his most private, in fact, his purely inward self-development lays the basis and forms the spirit out of which the rest of what he does goes out to the world around him and influences the spirit, life, and activity of the people around him.

*   *   *

Now, at the close of my exposition, I might be asked in which element of the Council's declaration on Christian morality I find the most special significance. Is it perhaps in the frankness and courage with which the Council—for the first time in the Church's history—made the far-reaching attempt to set forth the Christian view of the world and of man's coping with the world in the moral sphere? The Council did this in basic and highly pertinent individual questions in the Pastoral Constitution on the Church in the Modern World, and it was rightly congratulated for this achievement. Yet, I think the greater significance of the Council's statements on Christian morality lies elsewhere, namely, in their radical return to Christ and our own call in him; in this way the specifically Christian element of Christian morality was clarified. In this way also the radical character of Christian morality becomes apparent. That is to say: what is of prime importance is personal decision and personal responsibility, undertaken in love, in imitation of Christ. This is possible through, and necessitated by, the grace of Christ. All the concrete formation and organization of life and world must be an expression and 'mediation' of this fundamental moral reality. But this fundamental reality never really exists unless it is expressed visibly in the Christian structuring of one's life and world.

3   The Law of Christ[1]

Christian moral teaching, if it is to remain true to itself, must be careful not to give the impression that the Christian message and Christian existence are primarily a matter of ethics. The work of Christ is not meant to proclaim a higher moral standard, but rather salvation, which the love of the Father grants us through Christ. The work of him who first loved us, sending us his Son that we might live through him (1 *John* 4:9), should so permeate Christians that their lives and their life's work flow out from the fullness of salvation which was bestowed on them. In this way Christian morality will prove to be the Spirit of the Lord, a spirit which works primarily from within, where it lives as the gift of the Lord, and secondarily finds expression in the prescriptions and commandments which concern men and women who are called in Christ; both together, the Spirit of Christ, living and working in us, and the same Spirit, expressed in prescriptions and commandments, constitute the law of Christ.

What St Paul says of the new law of Christ as compared to the law of the Old Testament is said as *per typum*. Every law given by God is holy and divinely great (*Rom.* 7:12; 1 *Tim.* 1:8), but nevertheless is only leading to Christ (*Gal.* 3:24) and finds its fulfilment in him (*Rom.* 10:4). Now only Christ matters, the crucified and risen Christ; he is our salvation and our law (*Gal.* 6:2; 1 *Cor.* 9:21). No other law can be of

[1]Paper delivered at the Maynooth Union Summer School in Maynooth, Ireland, August 1964.

any value, unless it be subsumed in Christ and thus become the law of Christ. And it can only have been of value in history in so far as it virtually and fundamentally contained the law of Christ, as Thomas Aquinas says of the law of the Old Testament and of the natural law in its relation to the history of salvation.

When therefore at certain periods (not only in our days, but also, for instance, in the German theology of morals in the last century) Christian ethics become particularly conscious of their Christian character, they search for the Spirit of Christ, which should form our lives, this Spirit as we know it from the Scriptures, from tradition and from theology. Again and again the same twofold question is put to the current moral doctrine: (*a*) whether it is not based too exclusively on a philosophical anthropology, which sees man only as a being made to serve his Creator, and hardly at all as one who is lost in sin and receives justification and law from the Spirit of our Lord; (*b*) whether it does not stress too much a philosophical order, that is, an order of natural law, and neglects the Spirit of Christ, which after all determines the life of man, who has been born 'in the flesh' (*sarx*) in sin, but has been justified and saved 'in the spirit' (*pneuma*) in Christ. Within recent decades we have experienced such a re-appraisal with, on the one hand, its positive side, namely an enrichment through the appreciation of some Christian values often insufficiently perceived or, at any rate, reflected upon; and, on the other hand, its negative side, the danger of an unjustified exclusion of the absolute duty of the created being to its Creator and of the order of creation expressed in natural law.

Joy in Christ and in his law sometimes encourages the Christian to compare this law with the law of non-Christians, as if there existed a twofold moral law, one for Christians and another one for non-Christians, for the latter maybe even a purely natural law. Yet the conception which makes such a comparison, is guilty of an under-valuation of the law of Christ. Rather might one compare it with a purely natural moral law, if such a thing existed—which it does not. I agree that there is a natural order of creation, a natural moral law, but it does not stand by itself; it is part of the whole, the order and the law of Christ. Therefore, there is only one single law for all men, the law of Christ. It is the law for man, who is saved from the slavery of sin, justified by grace, and lives in the Church of our Lord. This is the human being and there is no other in the divine decree, except perhaps the one in whom (whether or not through his own fault) God's plan for man is only imperfectly realized, such as, for instance, the man who is ignorant, the sinner, the unbelieving man. Just as there is only one final destiny for all, which is to be heirs of the Father and co-heirs of Christ (*Rom.* 8:17; *Gal.* 4:6), so there is also for all only one way and one law which is Christ. Objectively, these are the facts, even though subjectively a man can and must pursue this way and live this law according to his subjective ability or, in other words, according to the degree in which he is near to Christ and knows him.

When we speak of the law of Christ, we must first of all pay attention to the fact that he himself, the person of Christ, is our law, the pattern of our life, its basis; secondly we must consider in which way and precisely in which sense Christ can truly be and is our law; and thirdly we must specially take note of the relation between the law of Christ and the moral natural law.

I. THE PERSON OF CHRIST AS PATTERN AND LAW

A true understanding of the plan of salvation, in the light of holy Scripture, enables us to see that the eternal God willed his Christ, the God-man, so that he could be the 'firstborn amongst many brethren' (*Rom.* 8:29). Therefore he let him be the 'firstborn from the dead' (*Col.* 1:18). He willed that all fullness should dwell in him and that so he should have the primacy (*Col.* 1:28; *Eph.* 1:22). Therefore, he is the fullness and original pattern of all who die to sin and are called to a new life.

Further, if in the light of an exegesis which is constantly gaining ground, we are to understand the Christ of the letter to the Colossians as the *Christus* and not only as the *Verbum,* then we see that this Christ, the God-man, was already the original picture, in whom and towards whom everything, particularly man, was created, so that he might be the 'firstborn of all creation', in whom and through whom all is created, and in whom all has its existence (*Col.* 1:15; cf. also 1 *Cor.* 8:6; *Eph.* 1:3–10). For all human and Christian existence, therefore, there is one, who is the archetype, and who as God-man contains in himself all true potentialities of human and Christian existence, namely Christ. From the beginning he was the one towards whom and according to whom all were created, so that he would be the first among many. At his entry into the world, his incarnation, he took into himself historically all human and Christian existence.

Therefore, he is the measure of life for all. Life means more than existing as man; it means living as Christ. One takes as the source and pattern of one's life the reality of Christ, the Son of God who became man, and who was crucified and glorified. Christ is for everyone the measure of his being and thereby also the measure of his life. He is the source and the measure of the grace that comes to everyone, and the source and measure of the being which this grace finds already in existence. For this reason he is for everyone the well-spring and pattern of supernatural morality (in relation to grace) and of natural morality (in relation to one's existence as mere man). When we circumscribe moral life with universal norms, natural and supernatural, we must not forget that these norms are, in the last analysis, derived from the God-man Christ, on whom all human being and all human order is based. If we seek to assess the individuality of each man and of the particular situation in which he finds himself, norms formulated in general terms do not satisfy us. We seek

the proper manner of applying these general norms. In this
search it strikes us that the individual and everything which
makes him a particular being—and so also the moral law
which applies to him—are founded on the one Christ. Von
Balthasar says quite rightly that our moral life should be
measured, in a more radical sense, by the person of Christ
rather than by general laws; that our moral duty is more
radically expressed as imitation of Christ rather than as
observance of general norms, which, of course, are presupposed in the imitation of Christ; and that one's own being
grounded on Christ is a more radical guide than universal
norms. Therefore, he calls Christ the most concrete norm,
because he is an individual person, and at the same time the
most universal norm, because he is the measure of each and
every person and of every situation.

Seen ontologically Christ is the archetype of each human
being, and each by his moral behaviour must endeavour to
reflect the Christ in whom he has his existence (*Col.* 1:17).
It is not enough to make it one's duty to realize certain moral
values or to fulfil abstract moral patterns, but each individual,
grounded on the person of Christ, must demonstrate the
meaning and value of his commitment. This is all the more
true in that Christ has given us, in a historical and approach-
able way, an example of human life, namely, his life, both
individual and conditioned by situations. This does not
mean that one who is not the individual Christ can repeat
this life—an impossibility—but one can imitate his example
in a particular way. We can love God in a way as he loves
God (*John* 15:10), and love our neighbour as he loved us
(*John* 13:34); we can even humbly serve our brother after
the example of the one who washed the disciples' feet (*John*
13:12–15); we can imitate his example of suffering (1 *Peter*
2:21) and his manner of walking on this earth (1 *John* 2:6).
We can, with the apostles (1 *Thess.* 1:6; 1 *Cor.* 11:1), make
Christ's ideas our own (*Phil.* 2:5; *Rom.* 15:1–3; *Rom.* 15:7);
and we can have in our life ever before our eyes the glorified
Lord who died and who was awakened from the dead

(*Rom.* 6) after a life of suffering (2 *Cor.* 1:5; *Phil.* 3:10), anguish (*Col.* 1:24), persecution (2 *Tim.* 3:12), patience (2 *Thess.* 3:5), truth (2 *Cor.* 11:10) and love (*Phil.* 1:8). Following his example, looking at him, we should imitate him in our way and thereby 'put him on' (*Rom.* 13:14). Being able to see and experience the individual example of the absolute, once-for-ever man Jesus Christ, allows us to understand more deeply and truly what is and should be our own personal life—the particular life which for each of us has been created in him and awakened in us out of our death. We can understand more deeply and truly what type of behaviour and what type of attitude is needed, so that any particular situation may be patterned on the original picture of the person of Christ.

Moreover the Christ, who is our archetype and example, has extended to us personal communion with himself so that we can follow him and can share in his destiny (death and resurrection: *Rom.* 6; *John* 12:26; 17:14). In order to make it a true discipleship and union of life, he gives us his life and resurrection as our possession (*Rom.* 6), he allows his life (the true vine) to be our life (*John* 15:5) and he makes us the members of his one body, whose head he is (*Col.* 1:18). The Christian who knows this community with the Lord, and who is aware of the call to personal following, the call of him 'who first loved me and gave himself up for me' (*Gal.* 2:20), will learn from the love in which he follows the Lord. This love will teach him, better than an ethic of values or a code of rules, to understand the example of the Lord and the meaning of his own life, a life which is based on the person of Christ as its personal archetype and standard.

II. THE LAW OF CHRIST AS GRACE AND CHALLENGE

Christ is the standard for the individual human person, for his life and his individual situation in life, since everyone is formed after the God-man Christ. This applies to the individual's concrete mode of existence as a human being, each in his own way and with a particular relationship to his environment; it applies also to the special way in which one has become a sharer in the grace of Christ. We must view grace as giving the highest and final determination to man's being, and so also to his activity. The grace-given being-in-Christ of each individual is being and task, fact and obligation, at once. The grace of Christ, considered as the last and highest form of being and the pattern for each one, cannot be taken in an empty and abstract way. It must be viewed as grace forming the individual man, or rather this particular man who comes to the highest fulfilment for which he exists through this precise grace of Christ. The grace of Christ, therefore, as pattern of each one, embraces in the same way also the pattern given in the concrete being of man, precisely as man, that is, the purpose of each individual given to him by natural law. The law of Christ is for this reason an inward law, namely the task imposed on us by our existence in Christ.

Yet grace, especially in the man who shapes his life in a personal and responsible way, must not be understood primarily as something which is in itself. Rather we must see it as power, as the effective activity of the holy Spirit in us. In this way it becomes clearer than ever how Christ is our law. The Spirit of Christ in us overcomes the demand of the flesh, the egoistical concupiscence of man under original sin, and forms in its place the spiritual man, the man who makes the innermost surrender by striving to be in his own daily life the 'man in Christ', which he is by the life of Christ.

The grace of the holy Spirit puts love in the place of the egoism which is caused by original sin. By a deep inner impulse this love presses towards a full personal realization of human and Christian existence, through which one is grounded in Christ. Therefore, the driving force of our lives as men and as Christians, the driving force of natural and supernatural being, will be felt not as a law which forces us against our inclination (particularly as man under original sin) and in this sense as an outer law. Rather will this driving force be felt as our innermost willing and loving, which is caused in us by the Spirit of Christ of which we are sharers. It is above all in this special sense that the law of Christ is an inner law. To man under original sin, as such, it is not only the law imposed from outside by legislation that appears to him as something contrary and to that extent an outward law; he also finds contrary and outward the law which corresponds to his own being (and is in this sense an inner law, that is, the law of natural and supernatural existence). As long as man remains in the life of the flesh he will more or less remain in this state.

If one is carried by the grace of the Spirit of Christ, the imperative of being man-in-Christ will be one's own willing and loving. The more one allows oneself to be caught up by the grace of Christ, the more will this imperative, which is based both on natural law and the supernatural order, become one's own innermost concern, one's inner law. What constitutes the law of Christian life and conduct, is not so much the being and obligation that are derived from Christ, but rather the striving and loving that flow from the grace of the Spirit of Christ.

The grace of the Spirit of Christ imparts to us above all a participation in the life of Christ, that is, a participation in the love of Christ, with the result that we love as Christ loves. In this way we can describe the love of Christ, which is activated in us by the grace of the holy Spirit, as the real and inner law of Christ. Whatever this driving love in us, the love of Christ, is able to carry out, is good; and only that is good which can be an expression of this Christian love, which is given to us by grace. One thing is clear, however: Christian love in us can carry out and express itself in what truly corresponds to and is demanded by our concrete human existence in Christ, only in so far as this is grounded in the person of Christ. Included in this is the natural law challenge to the individual human being, together with the supernatural demands arising from the

order of grace. There is question not only of the general
requirements of existence according to the natural and
supernatural moral order, but also of the concrete demands
which follow for each one from the impulsion and call of
grace, that the living Spirit of Christ makes active in us.
This love, which unites us with God, will have made on it
many a call and demand which will surpass the ordinary
demands of reason set by the natural law and the ordinary
demands of love. In any case all demands made on a believing
and loving Christian—even those grounded in natural law—
will be understood, willed and made real not only in their
own being, but beyond this—at least implicitly and without
reflection—as modes of living in Christ before the Father.

Christ therefore becomes law in us, not only in that he in
himself and in his formation in us is our ontological measure
and pattern, but in that he gives us from within by the action
of the grace of his Spirit the capacity to will and to love
according to this pattern. Christ is our law not so much in
acting and demanding from outside (in ways which counter
the desires of the man of the flesh), but rather in shaping and
guiding the inner man. He is lawgiver not so much because
he himself becomes a standard for us, or makes demands of
us, but because he overcomes the 'man of the flesh', and
causes in us by grace the fulfilment love demands. Grace is,
therefore, in each man the 'Spirit of life in Christ Jesus'
(*Rom.* 8:2), which pours out love in us (*Rom.* 5:5), which
helps our weakness (*Rom.* 8:26), and which moves us from
within (*Rom.* 8:14). The grace of the Spirit of Christ therefore is the law of Christ, because it (1) enlightens the
Christian so that he can understand the Christian challenge
and the call of Christ to each one, and (2) it gives the love
which accepts and lives the call of Christ. The grace of the
Spirit of Christ is not a law set forth before all men in the same
way, but an internal guide and thereby a law for each single
person from within.

This grace is not just a law that remains within the general
pattern of universal norms, but a law that leads step by step

towards perfection, the fullness of Christ. The law of Christ does not only command this and that particular thing in the same way to all people. It challenges each person entirely according to his possibilities in his particular situation in life under the call of grace.

The law of Christ is primarily grace. As such it enlightens each one, moves him from within and thereby leads him to the perfection which is due to him singly. This law of Christ, as has been said, is not contrary to any outer law, but includes it. The natural moral order, grounded in the being of man, retains its absolute validity under the dynamic force of grace, and the same can be said of the supernatural moral order grounded in our existence in Christ. The commandments in the order of creation (in natural law), which can be formulated and are formulated, and the commandments of the gospel, as also the positive valid precepts of human authority, all these keep their value within the law of Christ. Yet they are not its primary elements. In themselves they remain outward laws, that is, both the demands of natural law and of the Christian law of love, in the sense that we cannot love and live them from within—all the more so, if we remain still 'men of the flesh' in spite of grace. Thus they are still a law bringing sin and death. Only the grace of the Spirit of Christ makes them our inner law, so that we love and live them and thereby live as Christ lived. Again they are only an outward law in the sense that they cannot give a complete picture of how each one is led by grace to the perfection which Christ has destined for him.

This secondary element of the law of Christ—distinct from the grace of the Spirit of Christ—the outward law, stands in the closest relation to its primary element, grace. It indicates values and ways of acting in which the impelling power of grace, the love caused by the holy Spirit, will express itself. The commands of the moral order, which are formulated or could be formulated, show this or that as the task of true human and Christian living. This is their intrinsic meaning. Over and above this, they have a self-transcending sense, for Christ's guidance by grace and Christian love will be a driving force only within these commands and not outside them. They show the Christian who loves God and is led by the holy Spirit, a way which he must never leave. As outwardly formulated commands they help us to avoid error. We are limited by our condition as *viatores* and by the tendencies of the 'fleshly' man, which we will always remain in this life. The commandments will help us not to misunderstand the driving power of grace and love, not to interpret it in the manner of a man of 'flesh' and try to realize it in this manner. In this way the outward law is a help and a salutary constraint, serving the primary element of the law of Christ, the grace of the Spirit of Christ within.

Therefore, the Christian moral code will effectively expound, unfold, motivate, and make understandable the commands of the law of Christ, of the gospel and of the natural order of creation for all Christians and non-Christians. In this way it becomes a guide to the true man and the man-in-Christ. It will point to the person of Christ so that knowing the archetype, and the historical example, and lovingly imitating the Lord who is united with us by grace, we can grasp more deeply the value of the prescriptions and commands. Christian moral teaching must also make clear that even the person of Christ and the demands based on the person of Christ would become for us men under original sin, sin and death, were it not for the working of the grace of the Spirit of Christ within us. We can also see that the Lord, leading us within, will indeed move us to an absolute or unchanging observance of his prescriptions and commands. At the same time he will move each individual person along a way towards Christian perfection, which is for him alone. He will lead each on to his particular perfection, which is grounded in the person of Christ and on the call of Christ. Even if the guidance of grace within us and the love caused by God within us do not move us away from the prescriptions of moral order and from precepts, loyalty to these prescriptions and commands must not endanger loyalty to the grace within us. For this grace points to the appropriate manner, spirit and intensity in which the prescriptions and commandments are to be fulfilled by each individual; it points also to something higher than the general order and general rules and commands.

Loyalty to order and pattern, as the secondary element of the law of Christ, must not turn us away from the primary element, the inward grace of the Spirit of Christ, which alone brings about Christian life and its *fulfilment*. This grace within, which in each individual overcomes gradually the 'fleshly' man, is a personal guidance by the Spirit of Christ and leads the 'spiritual' man on progressively step by step. The systematic setting forth of the prescriptions and commands must not claim to be absolute, but should be done so as to respect the freedom in which the Lord leads and calls each one. This, however, will not be outside law and order.

III. THE LAW OF CHRIST AND NATURAL LAW

The question of the natural order of creation, the law of nature, stood out prominently in the treatment of the law of Christ, and had necessarily to stand out, because we had to prove that the Christian moral order lies in the God-*man*. It is of importance to set forth now, expressly, the position of the natural law in relation to the law of Christ.

It is clear that the moral natural law belongs as an integral part to the whole of the Christian moral law. This is clear from the fact that, for instance, both Christ himself and St Paul, neither of whom intends anything but the propagation of Christian morality, press for an observance of natural morality. St Paul propagates the commands of natural morality as belong to the *Evangelium* (gospel) of the Lord (1 *Thess.* 4:2; *Phil.* 4:9; 1 *Cor.* 7:10). The Church of Christ includes in its preaching, interpretation and defence of the Christian moral teaching, the natural order of creation also. The Christian existence and Christian ordering of our life is founded in Christ as the God-man, and in the fact that the Word of God, entering into the world, became man and thereby our archetype and model (example). Man thus finds himself in an order of things grounded in human nature as such. For this reason, as already remarked, the grace of the Spirit of Christ within us compels us to loyalty to the order of creation.

The natural moral law has a definite place within the Christian moral law. In the God-man his 'being man' should be seen as a substratum, enabling God's Word to dwell amongst us in a human way. Grace and God's revelation presuppose as their 'substratum' human nature, so that we can well (possibly) assume that 'being man' is willed by God as ordered to 'being under grace' or 'being in Christ'. Therefore *quoad se* it is not the natural law which is primary, but the Christian moral law which necessarily implies the natural law, which is, in fact, presupposed by the supernatural law in itself. *Quoad nos*, however, the primary place will always be held by the law of nature, to which we see added other moral elements, derived from the supernatural order, from the Word incarnate, from the individual call of grace (*natura, non re, posterius*). To these elements we have no approach except under the supposition of the natural order of creation.

Within the Christian moral order, the natural law has an immanent meaning that is specific to itself. The natural law speaks of a true human existence and of human values. But because its position is within the order of Christ, it has not only a meaning proper to itself but also a *transcending* meaning—at least if we look at it abstracting from its being in Christ. Concretely, *quoad se* (that is, in the totality of creation, which is precisely not only natural but in fact grounded in Christ) it must not only serve to make one the true human being as such, but before all else the Christian being which obviously demands and includes in itself true human existence. The man who is in fact in Christ, always intends in his behaviour within the natural law more than this natural law, even if he does so without reflection. In it he refers always to Christ, to God the Father, to salvation. He achieves in his conduct according to the natural law something beyond that law, because he does it with an intention that goes beyond the natural level. Acting according to natural law therefore gains, if done 'in Christ', real salvific power, which in itself, abstractly taken, it cannot have.

Examining salvation from the historical viewpoint, one can with good reason say that Christ has redeemed the natural law. Natural law in this sense is an inner inbuilt law; it consists primarily not of outward norms, but is an order particular to man himself, towards which man is fundamentally inclined as right and reasonable. To the man of original sin, in so far as he thinks and strives in a 'carnal' way, the demands of the natural law are disagreeable. They become for him, as we said before, sin and death. They are for him demands from without. The grace of the Saviour, the Spirit of Christ within us, turns the natural law to a law of life in that it changes us to men of the spirit, who fulfil lovingly the natural moral order in a Christian life. Over and above this the Spirit of Christ helps us—by revelation, Church and grace—to come to the knowledge of the natural order of creation; because this knowledge is placed in jeopardy, largely because of the consequences of the Fall. The continuous activity of the Spirit of Christ concerning the natural law, its knowledge and fulfilment, shows us how correct it is to see the natural law in the whole of the work of salvation and in the corresponding law of Christ, because the supernatural activity of grace, revelation and Church does not take place for human existence as such.

If we look at the moral order of man as such, namely the natural law, we must never forget that we talk of something in the abstract when we isolate it from complete reality, from the law of Christ. Then we understand that the natural law does not really refer to *natura pura* (which, just as *natura lapsa* and *natura redempta*, expresses a definite condition or

G

state of the human being, namely the merely natural state). It refers rather to the specific nature of man, independently of any particular state in which it happens to be realized. This is important for the question of a continuity or discontinuity between natural law and the law of Christ. Is there then a contradiction between these two? Is the natural law being altered under Christ? The fact that certain demands, for example, those of the Sermon on the Mount, are perceived by us as difficult and demanding sacrifice—and this they certainly are—is due not so much to any tension between the law of Christ and the natural law, as to tension between the law of Christ and the carnal man. The carnal man immediately rebels, and the selfishness imparted by original sin must be corrected by sacrifices before he can fulfil the due order. Man redeemed from the depths of fallen nature will, however, sacrifice genuine human values, precisely in order to attain the lofty level of Christian existence. These values, however, are those of an order of pure nature (*natura pura*). But in fact man has not been created for the condition of pure nature, but essentially to be open to every call of God. He has been created in accordance with the Creator's will, with a view to his fulfilment in Christ. A natural law measured by the standard of *natura pura* must find itself limited and reduced by the gospel; a natural code of ethics measured by the standard of *natura*, of human existence as such, finds in Christ its true fullness of meaning, for which God had intended it from the beginning. It would, therefore, be more correct not to speak, as often happens, of a comparison between the law of Christ and a purely natural ethical order, but rather of the relation of the law of Christ to the natural order of creation, to natural law.

The law of Christ is more than a code of natural law demands; but even the natural law order, when seen in the totality of the law of Christ, goes beyond, transcends itself. By the law of Christ is meant the ethical order which is grounded in the person of Christ and his image in the individual man. Yet the law of Christ is not only, not even primarily, an order which makes demands and has universal validity; it is rather the inner grace of the Spirit of Christ, which powerfully leads the individual to form in himself the image of Christ, and to form it in that full measure to which the Lord calls the individual.

4 Basic Freedom and Morality[1]

Whoever sets out to discuss man's freedom in the matter of moral conduct must be clear himself and make sure that his audience is clear, as to what sort of freedom he has in mind. Does he mean, for example, the psychological *freedom of choice* (*libertas arbitrii*), whose functioning in our aims, decisions and actions is capable of being generalized in a 'moral psychology'? Or does he mean the *moral freedom*[2] of the good man—the kind, considerate man, let us say—who has committed himself by this freedom to leading a good life, and who now possesses this freedom in action, that is, in his commitment of himself to doing good; and who may have even largely integrated in that decision the resistances inherent in his concupiscent human nature? Or is it a question of the *Christian freedom* mentioned by St Paul, that freedom which, through the dwelling within us of the Spirit of Christ, leads us to renounce our selfish, worldly inclinations and fix our minds on the things of the Spirit?

As a matter of fact the freedom we have in mind here is not the psychological freedom of choice nor moral freedom nor Christian freedom, but that contemporary concept called *basic freedom* (*liberté fondamentale*[3]) or *transcendental freedom* (K. Rahner[4]).

[1]Lecture at the Second National Congress of the Association of Italian Moral Theologians, Assisi, Italy. 16–19 April 1968.

[2]Cf. B. Schüller, *Gesetz und Freiheit*, Düsseldorf 1966, 26–30.

[3]See P. Fransen, 'Pour une psychologie de la grâce divine', *Lumen Vitae* (12) 1957, 209–40.

[4]*Passim*; e.g. in 'Theology of Freedom', *Theological Investigations* VI (tr. K. H. Krüger), 179–96. Cf. also J. B. Metz, 'Freiheit', in *Handw. theolog. Grundbegriffe* (H. Fries), I, 403–14.

It may be well at the outset to state briefly the relation between this basic freedom and the other freedoms mentioned above.

As regards *freedom of choice,* modern psychology attempts to sound the depths of the human ego in order to discover the ultimate principle that governs man's actions and the aims he pursues, and the extent to which these aims and actions are freely chosen. Basic freedom, on the other hand, denotes a still more fundamental, deeper-rooted freedom, not immediately accessible to psychological investigation. This is the freedom that enables us not only to decide freely on particular acts and aims but also, by means of these, to determine ourselves totally as persons and not merely in any particular area of behaviour. It is clear that man's freedom of choice and his basic freedom are not simply two different psychological freedoms. As a person, man is free. But this freedom can, of course, be considered under different aspects. A man can, in one and the same act, choose the object of his choice (freedom of choice) and by so doing determine himself as a person (basic freedom). True, when we consider freedom under this separate aspect of basic freedom, we run some risk of presenting a wrong picture of it, but, on the other hand, we come to grips at once with an element of personal freedom and morality that has not always had sufficient attention in moral theology.

Moral freedom may be directed towards particular virtuous acts or aims and may even, in its highest form, be equivalent to basic freedom exercised for the good. Basic freedom can, of course, also be exercised negatively: it then becomes the opposite of moral freedom—the voluntary enslavement of the selfish ego.

Christian freedom, the freedom of the spiritual man spoken of by St Paul, is in fact basic freedom and self-determination exercised in the grace and under the guidance of the holy Spirit.

Our inquiry into basic freedom obviously presupposes the conviction that it is not the good and the evil aims and actions in themselves or the measure of good in man's exercise of his freedom of choice that determine his goodness or wickedness. Here the decisive factor is rather the extent to which an individual as a person, in his freely chosen good or evil aims and actions, determines himself as a whole, i.e., in basic freedom, thus determining himself as good or evil, and ordering his aims and acts in accordance with that determination. The question of basic freedom, therefore, ultimately becomes the question of the moral goodness and wickedness of man.[5] It will be dealt with here under four heads:

I. Basic freedom and man as person.
II. Basic freedom and freedom of choice.
III. Basic freedom and self-awareness.
IV. Basic freedom and grace.

I. BASIC FREEDOM AND MAN AS PERSON

Basic freedom stands for our freedom in so far as it enables us to ascertain not only the morality of particular aims and actions but also the morality of the person who pursues or performs them. It brings home to us, accordingly, the full meaning of morality. Our first task, then, will be to inquire into the relation between basic freedom and man as person.

[5]The activation of basic freedom takes place as a basic decision (*option fondamentale*). There is an extensive bibliography on this in H. Reiners, *Grundintention und sittliches Tun*, Freiburg/Br. 1966; J. Maritain, *Neuf leçons sur les notions premières de la philosophie morale*, Paris 1949, 119–28; Z. Alszeghy and M. Flick, 'L'opzione fondamentale della vita morale e la grazia', *Gregorianum* (41) 1960, 593–619; P. Fransen, *art. cit.* (note 3 above); J. B. Metz, 'Befindlichkeit', in *Lex. f. Theol. u. Kirche*, 2 111, 102–4. While we regard the basic decision as a mature act of self-determination, others (e.g. Fransen) understand it more as a preliminary, as yet immature, groundwork. On the other hand, we do not understand by it an almost definitive decision (Maritain's formulations are too one-sided for us), but an act that grows and deepens, that can, however, also become blunted and can even be turned into its opposite.

The ultimate objective of our inquiry will be to obtain an answer to the question: what does the freedom of myself as a *person* amount to, over and above my actions and my aims? Granted that my ego, that dynamic unity which is myself, is more than the sum of my acts and aims and that the latter are but the fitful expression and manifestation of the ego and not the personal ego itself, what is the morality of my personal ego, over and above the morality of my various actions?

Individual moral acts and aims are the object of moral knowledge and volition on the part of the person who performs or pursues them; they proceed from the person's objective, categorical knowledge and volition. But the personal ego can function not only in objective, categorical knowledge and volition but is itself—as subject—knowledge and freedom. For knowledge and freedom, so far as I myself as a person am concerned, are inextricable parts of that integrated, dynamic organism. A person is conscious of himself as a subject without reflecting on himself as an object. As a subject a person is committed in freedom without realizing himself in action as an object. This self-consciousness—consciousness of himself—and freedom, of the person as a subject, evidently lie much deeper than the subconscious or the unconscious as understood by psychologists, because the subconscious and the unconscious are categorically and objectively defined.

What then do we mean by self-consciousness and self-determination of the person as a subject? Now this person with which we are dealing is the human person and the human person is not a monad turned in upon, and locked up in, itself. On the contrary the human person is by its very nature oriented towards other human persons, obviously not to ward them off but to enter into relations with them. (We can be sure that no man is an island!) Self-realization in openness towards others—love—is the true moral commitment of the basic freedom of the person; withdrawal into oneself is negative self-commitment. Finally, basic freedom enables us, indeed presses us, to place ourselves as persons unreservedly at the disposal of him who has the greatest claim on us, because he—who is God—created us as persons.

The reason why *basic* freedom or *transcendental* freedom is so called will now be clear. The free self-commitment of ourselves as persons is more than any particular action or actions and more than the sum of them; it underlies them, permeates them, and goes beyond them, without ever being actually one of them.

A man's free and basic self-commitment, consisting ultimately of the gift or refusal of the self in love to God, should not be equated with any particular moral act. The act of basic freedom is the realization of the person as a whole. He means to follow out his intention to its ultimate depth and intensity, and to build into it every particular personal development in time and space, past and future. Love of God—the positive act of basic freedom—would not amount to this effort to commit the entire person if the person were content with a minimum of self-giving, or were indifferent to past moral failure or to conversion to concrete good behaviour in the future, or took no trouble to integrate the resistant forces of human concupiscence. Self-realization in basic freedom is thus a total act, in so far as it means the self-determination of the person as a whole in face of God's total demand upon him. On the other hand this self-commitment of the person as a whole in basic freedom is always immature and imperfect, not a complete self-commitment of the whole person, since it can become deeper and more intensive, has to be maintained and made manifest in countless different situations, and has to prevail against the still continuing hostile tendencies of the concupiscent ego. Similarly the negative use of basic freedom, the closing of the self against God, is still not a total disposal of the entire person. Here too not every possibility of self-determination is realized, not all of the past is worked through and absorbed, not all the tendencies towards good that remain are integrated. And when will the realization of the person as a whole, for good or ill, finally be total, complete, and thus definitive?

One should not think of the person in his basic freedom as pure possibility, as if one day he discovered his basic freedom and with it the possibility of self-determination and then was able to consider, while in possession of himself simply as a free person, how he should commit himself. No one exists simply in the *possibility* of basic free decision, since an adult has already come to freedom, a freedom that is already in action, has become a self already freely engaged.[6] Basic freedom exists only in the concrete act. The mature adult who has grown into created freedom, has already decided upon the meaning of what life requires of him, whether to be open or closed to the absolute demand God makes of him. This basic freedom of a person as a whole in face of the Absolute should not be confused with freedom of choice in particular moral acts. It must be understood that we are basically free always and only as loving or sinning—but loving or sinning freely.

Accordingly we are never undecided about the ultimate meaning of our existence, which is either a total surrender of the self to the Absolute, or a refusal of such surrender. Moreover this does not mean an act of surrender in the past, but a continuing activation of our basic freedom. It is clear that this continuing free activation in a particular moral direction is a fundamental force in the moral formation of our life, as it takes shape in successive acts (H. Reiners, *Grundintention*[7]). If moral life follows the line of the basic free option, this is further developed and strengthened. If it takes the opposite direction, either as a superficial inconsistency or as a fundamental free choice, then this means not simply the self-commitment of a hitherto neutral person, but a contradiction of the self already freely activated.

[6]Cf. the work already cited, J. B. Metz, 'Befindlichkeit' (note 5 above).
[7]See note 5.

II. BASIC FREEDOM AND FREEDOM OF CHOICE

Obviously there exists a significant interaction between the basic free option of the person as a whole and the particular moral acts and efforts that to a greater or lesser extent derive from freedom of choice.

We speak of freedom of choice in so far as we are able, in particular acts, to apply ourselves freely to the many possibilities and requirements of life as it unfolds before us in space and time. We must choose freely to be just, loyal, merciful, and so on. The moral act of free choice can be expressed in an external act, or in an inner act of free will. But when we bring to realization, in our free choices, the values of justice, loyalty, mercy, and so on, at the same time we engage ourselves as persons. The personal realization of justice, loyalty and mercy through free choice always means an effort to engage the person as a whole in basic freedom. Only to the extent that justice and loyalty and mercy constitute a striving for the self-realization of the person are they in fact moral at all. And only where justice and loyalty and mercy express and signify the person who is truly acting in basic freedom, only there are they moral in the full and real sense. So long as they are 'merely' personal, but do not spring from a true commitment of the person, they are indeed moral acts, but only by analogy and not in the full sense. [8]

Conversely there can be no particular, categorical act of basic freedom—for a person can never grasp and engage the totality of himself categorically, as an object. As soon as the self, as subject, grasps at the self as object, the subjective self that acts is no longer to be found within the self confronting it as object. Therefore the basic, free self-realization of the subject always takes place in particular acts related to an object distinct from the person as a whole. The spiritual person can only attain basic, free self-realization when he

[8]Cf. B. Schüller, 'Zur Analogie sittlicher Grundbegriffe', *Theologie und Philosophie* (41) 1966, 3–19.

emerges from his spiritual unity into the physically conditioned diversity of his development in space and time, to
which his personal freedom of choice is directed.

The various free moral acts are accordingly a constitutive
element of self-realization in basic freedom, but at the same
time they are also—at least in themselves—a sign of this
self-realization. They are particular acts of free choice—
justice or loyalty or mercy—which express and derive from
the total act of basic freedom, the radical opening out of the
self to the Absolute. Only, of course, 'in themselves'. For
particular acts of free choice can also spring from a more
superficial level of the personality and not express its basic,
freely chosen attitude. A trivial lie, for example, does not
derive from the fundamental decision of the man who loves
God.

If we are right to consider and assess separately the two
aspects of our freedom—basic freedom and freedom of
choice—then it follows that the actual value of a moral act
depends more on the basic free self-commitment of the person
than on the various virtues arising out of free choice. The
real value of morality lies in a person's self-commitment in
relation to the Absolute. Of course this is realized and
demonstrated in freely chosen virtuous acts which specify
categorically the transcendental self-commitment of the
person. Conversely the proper use of basic freedom can only
occur and be made plain in an act which is specified as
morally good.

It is accordingly love that lends merit to the particular
moral act of justice, loyalty or mercy which it fills and
penetrates. It is not justice and loyalty and mercy as such
that are meritorious, but only justice, loyalty and mercy as
expressing the gift of self to the Absolute. The specific act
of free choice—justice, loyalty, mercy—may be carried out
as a *preliminary* movement towards God without true self-
commitment (love) for him. But the particular act of free
choice is only meritorious if it expresses the real commitment
of the self in an act of basic freedom, that is love. When the

Church's teaching authority lays down that not only love, but also justice and other moral acts earn merit (DS 2455 f.), what is meant is this: not only a specific act of love of God freely chosen is meritorious, but also a specific act of other virtues, pre-supposing that it is permeated with the transcendental exercise of the love of God in basic freedom.

Here we can see again that the relationship of the various moral virtues to the virtue of love corresponds to the relationship of specific free choice to basic freedom. The love that commits a person as a whole is not a specific act of love distinct from other specific moral acts, but a transcendental self-commitment in basic freedom that is realized and demonstrated in particular specific acts of free choice. When Christ both distinguishes between his disciples' love for him and their keeping of his word and also sees the two as one, so that love indeed includes the keeping of his word and the observance of his commands (*John* 14:15, 21, 23), this really means the same thing. It is not a specific act of love but the transcendental love acting out of basic freedom that necessarily lives and expresses itself in the keeping of his word through the various acts of free choice. This difference between the person as a whole, whom we have at our disposal in basic freedom, and the person's acts, which we determine by free choice, is also meant when Scripture says that God looks not only at a man's deeds but also at his heart, that the holy Spirit by grace gives us a new heart; and this is the sense wherever the biblical speech of the Old and New Testaments uses the concept of the heart to signify the depths of the human person. It is, however, also a matter of the relation between basic freedom and freedom of choice when Paul speaks of sin in the singular and of sinful acts in the plural (*Rom.* 5–7), or when he interprets the many and various vices of the heathen as the expression of the single sin of culpable godlessness (*Rom.* 1:18–31). In the same way, according to John, every sin—all sins—are fundamentally this single sin: malice, that is, the self-sufficient rejection of God as the source of our salvation (1 *John* 3:4). For in all these texts the same theme seems to be dealt with, that is that the many sins of all kinds are really and ultimately more than they indicate in their specific classification: they express a man's fundamental free disposition of himself as a whole in face of the God of salvation, a total disposition therefore, that is present at the deepest level of the many individual sins.

A short reference should be made to a further phenomenon of freedom in the moral life, that concerns the relation between basic freedom and freedom of choice. The man who is realizing himself in basic freedom and in freedom of choice builds up for himself in the many specific fields of morality certain fundamental tendencies—virtues and vices. That means immediately and above all that the will to follow a particular good or bad course of conduct, freely chosen, is and continues to be activated in such a way that good and bad acts will follow as a result of the freedom thus activated, and continuing to be activated. Secondly, it means that practice increasingly integrates the various layers of a man's being with his freely-chosen basic tendency of conduct (virtue or vice), so that the performance of individual acts meets with less resistance. Freedom activated in virtue or vice, that is moral freedom, does not give rise to particular acts in such a way, it seems to us, that they are only free because of the freedom (moral freedom) that has already been set in motion. For so long as man is a pilgrim (viator) and his freedom has not yet been definitively committed, freedom of choice is always required for individual free acts. Only in this way can it be understood how there is the possibility of intensifying or moderating basic tendencies, and even the possibility of choosing freely in contradiction to a free basic tendency. (Thus indeed the basic freedom that has been activated can also be re-activated and reaffirmed, or can even be turned around in an opposite direction.)

A short reference should be made to a further meaning of the relationship between basic freedom and freedom of choice. Every world view, so long as it is fully human, has its origin in those depths of the person in which knowledge and freedom are indivisible, in man's commitment of himself as a person. The formation of a world view takes place basically in responsibility and therefore in moral acts—these, however, are grounded, as acts of free choice, fundamentally in the person as such, acting in basic freedom. Basic freedom expresses itself in the world through freedom of choice, but in a world that shows itself to be a world of human persons.

Obviously there exists in moral life an interdependence between basic freedom and freedom of choice. Above all, morality in the true and full sense only exists, as we have said, where our freedom, as basic freedom and freedom of choice, simultaneously determines our action. The basic freedom of personal self-commitment can be activated only in acts of free choice. Such acts, however, when they do not correspond to the depths of self-commitment in basic freedom, are not moral in the real and full sense, but only by analogy. For not every act of free choice necessarily corresponds to that self-commitment of the person—even when the moral quality of the act is recognized and its commission freely willed. A lie, recognized in its sinfulness, considered and freely willed, does not usually determine a self-commitment of opposition to God in basic freedom; for the intrinsic opposition to God of the lie, the No before God, which is always grave in itself, is in practice usually not sufficiently evaluated and is therefore not personally realized as such. An exceedingly large gift of alms by a sinner, made in full knowledge and freedom, will very often express the beginning of change in him, often too, but by no means necessarily and always, true conversion in basic freedom from sinner to lover. Thus both the materially costly act of almsgiving and the materially light act of lying remain, seen in personal terms, 'light', 'superficial' acts, moral acts only by analogy, because the self-commitment of the person in basic freedom does not enter into them. Many of our daily good or bad deeds do not involve the self-commitment of the person as a whole in basic freedom and are therefore—as acts only of free choice—merely 'light' moral acts, acts performed at the surface level of the person, moral acts by analogy.

We are accustomed to dividing moral acts into those that are fully human (*actus perfecte humani*) and those that are not (*actus imperfecte humani*). Is it in fact sufficient to let fully human acts be defined solely by clear knowledge concerning their morality and their performance in free choice? In that sense the lie, and also the costly alms of the sinner who has not yet been converted, are fully human actions. But is this not to understand the *actus perfecte humanus* in an altogether too formal way? Must we not, in order to speak in real rather than formal terms, regard as the essential condition of a fully human act that it be the expression of the person's self-activation, in basic freedom, before the Absolute? But if we understand the *actus perfecte humanus* in this way, then it is always—whether good or bad—an *actus gravis,* a moral act in the true sense and not merely by analogy. Both the *materia levis* of the lie and the *materia gravis* of an exceedingly costly alms-gift can be realized without the activation of basic freedom. Is not occasionally a *materia levis* ('good' or 'bad'), perhaps some lack of love or small proof of love, realized in the simultaneous activation of basic freedom, that is, as a 'gravely' good or bad deed? Thomas took this to be the case when man made his first moral choice.[9] Others hold this to be possible for the mystics,[10] or at some point in the course of a long series of such actions:[11] when, that is, there comes about at the centre of the person full existential understanding and evaluation of the relationship of the person to the Absolute that is involved.

Let us make yet another, and final, remark concerning the mutal influence upon each other of basic freedom and freedom of choice, which indeed has already been briefly

[9]*S. theol.* 1–11, q. 89, a. 3; and *passim.* Cf. Maritain, *op. cit.* (note 5).

[10]Thus e.g. B. Häring, *The Law of Christ,* 1, Cork 1967, 362.

[11]Thus K. Rahner, 'Gerecht und Sünder zugleich', *Geist und Leben* (36) 1963, 434–45; H. Rondet, *Notes sur la théologie du péché,* Paris 1957, 111 f.

touched upon. The free choice and realization of good or
bad acts and the creation by free choice of good or bad
tendencies may decide or occasion the intensification or
diminution of the basic intention arising out of basic freedom,
and even indeed the reversal into its opposite—always
according to whether they correspond to or contradict the
basic intention. Total lack of concern in the sphere of venial
sins will diminish love of God (the basic intention) or could
even endanger it. The sinner's renewed attention to the
fulfilment of good will lessen his abandonment to evil and
clear a way for his conversion in basic freedom. Conversely
basic freedom will have its influence upon the performance
of free choice. The man who, because of his self-commitment
in basic freedom, lives in grace and love will not come so
easily to serious sin as another who has not made the basic
decision of surrender to God. For he does not only have to
carry out the evil deed in free choice, but he has also to
reverse, in basic freedom, his basic free attitude to God.
Therefore it cannot be assumed that someone continually—
'seven times a day'—changes from mortal sin to the love of
God and *vice versa*, not only because of the bias of grace,[12] but
also because of the effective power of love. Where the specific
acts—grave sins or acts of sorrow—seem to indicate the
contrary, one has to deal with more or less free acts of choice
without the involvement of self-commitment in basic
freedom. That is to say, the person is presumably in a
continuous state either of sin or of justification.

III. BASIC FREEDOM AND SELF-AWARENESS

Obviously we are conscious in different ways of the
activation of basic freedom and the realization of freedom
of choice, although the activation of basic freedom is
performed not as a distinct act in itself but in and through an

---

[12]*De verit.* q. 27, art. 1 ad 9: 'quanvis per unum actum peccati mortalis
gratia amittatur, non tamen facile gratia amittitur; quia habenti gratiam non
est facile illum actum exercere, propter inclinationem in contrarium.'

act of free choice. The problem to which we must now turn is that of awareness of the activation of the person as a whole in basic freedom.

That there is an awareness of basic, free self-commitment can hardly be questioned, since a free process can only be a conscious one. While, however, the performance by free choice of a particular moral action makes possible an objective knowledge of this—whether it be more in a conceptual and reflexive or more in an intuitive manner—this is not possible in relation to the person's basic and free activation to love or to sin. We have already noted that objective reflection on the self can never take in the whole self as subject; the subjective 'I' which reflects and acts in this reflection remains, precisely as such, outside the 'I' that is the object of reflection. It cannot be fully established by my objective reflection whether I am lover or sinner in fulfilment of basic freedom. There can be no adequate objective knowledge of this matter. This corresponds to the declaration of the Council of Trent (DS 1534 f.), that no one has a certain knowledge of the state of grace—and that indeed means also of his basic free love of God. And yet basic free self-commitment—love and sin—cannot be other than conscious—precisely because it is an act of freedom. This consciousness is not objective, or even reflexive, but transcendental and unreflexive. The person acting in basic freedom is totally present to himself,[13] not as object but as subject, not perceived but self-aware, not seen from outside but experienced in himself.

The same consideration applies when Scripture, as well as our own reflection, leads us to distinguish between love as total surrender and good works, as also between sin (in the singular) as refusal of surrender to the God of salvation, and sins (in the plural) as evil works. In the objective and reflexive consciousness of the man who carries out good works in grace and love, these good works—perhaps some

---

[13]Certainly the being present to himself of the person as a whole is not a consciousness in unbounded fullness, for the human spirit is a finite spirit.

H

service of love to his neighbour—are related to an act of free choice. If it were otherwise, if in his objective consciousness he referred to his self-commitment in loving God, then the good work for his neighbour would perhaps not be achieved, or would be experienced as less than true love of neighbour as such. Self-commitment in love is not specifically 'known', but transcendentally 'conscious'. This manner of perception is not less than the other but more deeply-rooted and richer. That too is why the man who, in his good works, reflects on his own act of love of God does not really see it in its fullness—as a transcendental process—but only a specific and inadequate expression of it. In the same way the sinner does not refer, objectively and reflexively, to his basic free self-commitment as he shuts himself off from God, but to the specific, freely chosen act of sin. Yet he is conscious of his refusal of love in basic freedom. The assertion often heard that sinners only want the sinful act but are not aware of any refusal of love of God and moreover, do not want this, overlooks the fact that the real and fundamental withholding of the self, because it is a commitment of basic freedom, takes place in the realm not of objective knowledge but of transcendental self-awareness.

What is said here also answers, basically, the question of how a person can really take a stand in relation to God in love or in sin as commitment of himself as a whole. In intensive good work, or in abandonment to sin, specific thinking about God tends more or less to disappear, though it somehow remains present as unreflecting awareness. But the decisive factor is something else: specific knowledge about God and the taking up of a specific attitude towards God by free choice do not constitute the really fundamental relationship to him. Deeper, more fundamental, is the transcendental—and therefore not objective—awareness of God as the absolute horizon of human reality. So also the surrender or the withholding of the self as a basic free act is not a specific but a transcendental process. And as we are inclined to assume that the atheist who, whether in good faith or in culpable suppression of the truth (*Rom.* 1:18), declares that he does not have to take a God into account, also has a transcendental awareness of God, we should equally be justified in thinking that his good works and evil deeds, too, if performed not only by specific free choice but also in transcendental basic freedom, represent a certain self-surrender, or its refusal, to the God of whom he is transcendentally aware.

The answer that the basic free activation of the person—love or sin—is known in a transcendental and unreflexive manner but is not adequately carried over into specific, reflexive knowledge, does not satisfy us. How and to what degree can basic free self-commitment be translated into our specific consciousness? What knowledge of this kind do we have of our sinfulness or of our life in grace? What do we mean by our explicit opinion or statement that we are 'in a state of grace and love' or 'not in a state of grace but of (mortal) sin'?

Thomas Aquinas[14] puts it that we come, in our specific consciousness, to a knowledge of the state of our soul—that is, of the basic free position of the person as a whole before the Absolute—by means of a 'conjecture'. He gives criteria for such a conjecture: the consciousness of joy in God or of contempt for the world, the experience of divine consolation, the certainty that one can remember no mortal sin. We should like to put it in another way: we can conclude from various signs in the realm of free choice what is the manner of our basic free commitment. The material gravity of a sin, for example, is a sign, and leads us to suppose that in the committing of this sin the activation of the person in basic freedom has also taken place. But the gravity of the matter is only a *sign,* and only *one* sign. Perhaps we can establish at the same time a lack of sufficient moral and existential perception, or a lack of consent. This lack of freedom of choice in carrying out the deed would be another sign. For

[14]See *S. theol.* 1–11, q. 112, a. 5c.

without the activation of free choice there is no activation of
basic freedom and thus no realization of one's own self.
'Conjecture', therefore, based on 'signs', gives us that moral
certainty with which we judge reflexively ourselves and
others, the moral certainty which is characteristic of and
adequate for our actions and conduct in the sphere of the
specific acts of daily life.

IV. BASIC FREEDOM AND GRACE

If the activation of the person's basic freedom is love or
sin, total self-giving or self-refusal in face of the Absolute,
we should not definitively abstract from this the fact that the
required self-surrender exists only in overcoming the egoism
of human concupiscence and in abandonment to God as
Father, after the example of his Son-become-man, that is,
that it is possible only in grace. Were it to be otherwise,
salvation would lie within a man's own power. Accordingly
the relationship between basic freedom and grace should be
briefly dealt with.[15]

Here we understand grace as that which justifies a man
and re-forms him in the pattern of the God-man. It is—in
the mature man—not a 'something' to be received passively,
but a gratuitous transformation of the person. It is the working of grace which commits the person in his totality, tears
him free of the egoistic course of human concupiscence and
makes him respond in loving self-surrender to the love of
God—after the manner of the incarnate Son of the Father.
The grace that achieves this is obviously not only offered but
also freely accepted grace. As, however, the loving self-
disposal of the person as a whole is the activation of basic
freedom, it comes about that the offer of grace occurs in that
centre of the person in which he is totally present to himself,
in undivided self-awareness and freedom. Precisely in this

---

[15]Cf. the works already cited of Alszeghy-Flick, Dianich and Reiners (note 5
above), also Fransen (note 3 above).

centre there takes place the acceptance or rejection of grace as the activation of basic freedom. Acceptance or rejection of grace are more than simple acts of free choice, a simple Yes or No. They are a self-commitment of the person as a whole. And the transforming grace of Christ is offered only in acts in which the person at the same time acts in basic freedom.

Accordingly specific, individual moral acts as such are not the acceptance or rejection of grace. Acceptance and rejection, as self-activation in basic freedom, occur much more *through* specific acts of free choice. And individual acts that are moral in the full sense, in which a man disposes of himself as a whole, are, rather, as specific and individual acts (justice, loyalty, mercy), the expression and outcome of the free acceptance or refusal (in basic freedom) of grace, and with it the effect of grace or the consequence of lack of grace.

If we are inclined to assume, following a well-founded theory, that the grace of Christ is offered also to the man, as an individual, who does not (specifically) know or recognize Christ[16]—otherwise how could he attain salvation?—then it follows for the non-Christian also that the call of grace is offered to him too in that centre of the 'I' in which the person is present to himself in a transcendental, unreflexive awareness, and disposes of himself. As he experiences it in non-specific consciousness, so he will accept or reject it in the same consciousness and in basic freedom, that is, in non-specific self-disposition. Thus his self-realization in basic freedom in making himself open to the Absolute is also acceptance of the grace of Christ and therefore in some sense Christian love of God—and his sinful closing up of himself within himself is a sin against the grace of Christ. The love that according to the saying of Christ enables us to keep his word, is the grace offered and accepted in basic freedom or else its effect. Sin (in the singular) which is present in all sins (in the plural) as their fundamental reality is the self-

[16]On this question cf. e.g. Karl Rahner's essay on the teaching of the Second Vatican Council on Atheism in *Concilium* (3), March 1967, 5–13.

sufficient refusal to accept the love of the God of our salvation that is offered us.

A further consequence follows from the fact that acceptance or refusal of grace comes about through activation of basic freedom. We are thinking of those people whose way of life does not conform at all to the moral standard. This can be the outcome of a basic negative decision, that is, of rejection of grace. But what if the far-reaching lack of psychological and social formation—one thinks of 'a-social' people—leads one rather to think that such conduct is far from corresponding to true freedom of choice? Then it is indeed not impossible that such people, despite their outwardly immoral and a-social way of life, have not refused the grace of Christ in basic free self-activation, but have accepted it—or, after willed failures, have accepted it anew.[17]

But with reference also to those unambiguously good and outstanding Christians who without doubt accept God's grace in basic freedom and strive to correspond to it in daily life, visibly and in all seriousness, some raise this question, and not without reason: if at some weak point in their life there are repeated failures, cannot sometimes the manner of their life as a whole become a sign that the individual failures do not always correspond to a rejection of grace in the depths of basic freedom—that such acts, perhaps, do not arise from sufficient freedom of choice?

Finally let us refer to the many daily sins and good works which remain only on the edge of personal commitment (venial sins and minor good works). Since they are 'superficial' and therefore moral only in an analogous sense, that is, causing no activation of basic freedom, such acts do not mean a simultaneous acceptance or refusal of grace. They may well be linked to the acceptance or refusal of grace in earlier acts. It is above all, when they lie along the line of the basic direction—as its 'superficial' expression—that they are 'superficial' signs and effects of grace freely accepted or refused.

[17] Cf. Karl Rahner, 'Der Christ und seine ungläubigen Verwandten', *Geist und Leben* (27) 1954, 171–84.

Grace, therefore, calls, and is accepted or refused, in the centre of the person. For this very reason the grace that transforms a man can influence him in every sphere. For the man activated in basic freedom seeks to integrate with his basic intention every part of his being and life. Thus grace makes its way from the centre of a man and his basic freedom into all areas of life, into the many acts of free choice and beyond these into the formation of the world.

* * *

It seemed to us important that in the discussions of moral theologians about man's freedom this central area of freedom which we term basic freedom should come to be more regarded. The concept of basic freedom must necessarily have arisen, in recent times, in connection with such other concepts as basic decision, basic intention, self-disposition, total decision, transcendental awareness, etc. Obviously all these classifications point in the same direction: what is visible in individual free acts and efforts is not the whole, not the essence, of morality. If modern psychology gives us information about freedom and lack of freedom in human behaviour, it is doing an inestimable service to the better judgement of man's morality. But beyond this help from psychology we need the insights of philosophical and theological anthropology—and the classification of 'basic freedom' belongs here—in order better to understand the phenomena respectively of morality and of Christian morality. Our brief exposition should have shown that such anthropological reflections have not only theoretical but also practical value.

5   Human, Humanist and Christian Morality[1]

My subject is Christian morality. The question, in what sense Christian morality is specifically Christian, is posed in a quite new way in face of the various tendencies that today carry the slogan of secularism and secularization.

What is to be understood by secularization and secularism has from time to time to be established and defined. The common and essential element in both tendencies consists in the autonomy which it is intended to give or restore to the world or to man as the centre of this world; or, to put it negatively, it consists in the liberation of the concept of man and the world from super-human and supernatural elements and dependencies that deprive man and the world of their true meaning and their relative autonomy. *Secularization* in the good sense, as it occurs also in the realm of Christian belief, contains a clear opposition to every mythical or pantheistic or sacral world-concept. It distinguishes clearly between the Creator and the world created by God and it asserts a meaning in this world which is in the real sense autonomous and internal to the world—even if this world with its relative autonomy is also dependent in its totality on God the Creator. It is precisely this dogma of the creation which enables us to distinguish clearly between the created world and the transcendent Creator God who, however, because he is transcendent and thus distinct from the world,

[1]Lecture given in the Institute 'Pro civitate christiana', Assisi, Italy, February 1967.

is at the same time most deeply immanent in it. Present-day *secularism,* on the other hand, emphasizes the purely human immanence of complete independence from the transcendence of a Creator God. Certainly there are differences here, too. There is atheistic secularism in the real sense. The secularism of today, however, is agnostic rather than atheistic. For agnostic secularism atheism proposes a metaphysical thesis no less than theism. For this reason many do not wish even to speak of atheism. There is also a secularism among those who call themselves Christians and who therefore specifically refer to Christ. Some of these are not in the true sense atheists; they accept a God, at least in faith, although they are perhaps philosophically agnostics in this respect. Some would even rather invoke the person of Christ than a real God, though they do indeed understand Christ as a historical phenomenon that moves us to new and personal reflections and to corresponding moral conduct.

Not infrequently one speaks of *humanism* instead of secularism. To be sure, there are also different notions of humanism, and humanism does not mean the same as secularism in every case. If the use of the word humanism is preferred here, it is always understood in the sense of a secularist humanism. The reason why the term humanism is given preference to the word secularism will be seen from what follows.

When we are speaking here of humanist morality, this is clearly distinct from a so-called human morality, that is, the morality of man as such, as I can conceive and consider him without explicit reference to Christianity.

But all talk of humanist and human morality should serve the one goal of understanding better what Christian morality really means, and indeed what the Christianity of Christian morality means. Knowledge of the true nature of Christian morality is most important for men who have to live in a world which thinks largely in humanist secularist terms. In addition, true dialogue with the man who thinks in humanist terms is scarcely possible without such knowledge of Christian morality. In what follows six aspects of our subject will be treated in succession:

1. Human morality; 2. Christian morality; 3. Christian morality and humanist morality; 4. Love as the highest moral value; 5. The dialogue with the humanist; 6. Human morality as natural law morality.

I. HUMAN MORALITY

Under the heading of human morality we are concerned explicitly with man's morality as man, that is, not with his morality in so far as he is Christian or humanist. One can also say that we are concerned with the *morality of the natural moral law,* which basically means the same thing. However, let the term *human morality,* or *morality of man as man,* be given preference. Accordingly there is excluded from the following considerations everything that we know only from God's revelation about man as he is. That does not mean that man experiences himself as pure man. For man experiences himself always as the man of salvation, the man under the grace of Christ. To be sure, man as such, without revelation and faith in this revelation, does not know that he exists always as a man of salvation and a man under grace.

It has already been noted that Christianity, with its dogma of the creation of the world, has contributed a great deal to a true secularizing of the world, and thus to a more real and true relationship of man to the world. It is known that the morality of the natural moral law, as it is represented in Christianity, is not independent of the concept of natural moral law of the *Stoa.* But if the Stoic concept was a pantheistic world-view, then the dogma of creation freed the world from its supposed sacralization and divinity, and allowed it to be simply itself, the world. So this world, with its structures, meaning and autonomy, is distinct from a transcendent God, but at the same time it is not independent of this God who is the transcendent, and precisely for this reason the immanent, God of the world. This conception has its consequences in the field of morality.

A first consequence is this: if one proceeds from the pantheistic natural law concept of the *Stoa,* then the world is something sacral, something divine. Consequently one may not, in this view of the world and of man, intrude upon the world and upon man's reality, precisely because these are sacral and divine. Without joking one can say that the conduct of the Beatles, in letting their hair grow, corresponds in an admirable and perfect manner to the Stoic concept of the natural moral law. The example is not invented but is expressly found in the Stoic writings on natural morality (see Epictetus I, 16): for the man who has his hair cut interferes with the natural course of human life. In opposition to this view of things, Christianity has begun to understand, in a slower and lengthier development, that the reality of the world and of man is something given into the hand of the human person who, as the image of God, is not forbidden to intrude upon this reality, but is called upon precisely to form it. It is man's task to grasp this world and also his own reality, and to attempt to unfold the possibilities that lie in this divinely created reality.

This conviction has developed more and more, especially in recent times. There are two main reasons for this. Primarily, man has come to a deeper understanding of himself as a person. To be a person does not mean subjection to non-personal realities, but dominion over them. Thus it comes about, secondly, that we experience how this world and man himself find themselves in a continuous and rapid development, and this above all under the influence of man himself. It is man who brings the world to development, and succeeds in activating the latent possibilities of the world and of man. The man who sees this development of the world and at the same time understands man as a person, also grasps that the reality of man and the world—everything that in the past or today has been called 'nature'—is not merely a teacher who conveys to us how we should naturally behave.

The reality we call *nature* is also matter in man's hands, to be formed and, one can say, humanized and personalized by him. A human morality in the true sense of the word sees the reality of the world, and sees man in the world as its centre, and sees man as a person. Therefore, this morality requires man to give his own imprint more and more to the world. And this means that he should work upon the world with his own reason and in the light of his own possibilities, and should increasingly form the world and increasingly give it the shape of his own self and of his own rationality. And that applies not only to the extra-human world, but also to that human reality which we today call nature, as distinct from person. For a truly human morality, moral action means nothing other than 'being human', 'being rational'. The whole of reality must be subjected to human reason; man has increasingly to give it rational form. The fact that man should shape the world, should give it the shape of human rationality, is based on the fact that every reality, including that of man, is created reality. That, indeed, is the meaning of the world and the task of man in the world, in so far as it is the work of God the Creator.

A human morality understood in this way will accordingly require that man take over responsibility for forming the world and making himself the centre of this world. When one speaks of man as the centre of this world, the world is obviously to be understood in its relative and immanent autonomy. If one looks at things in their *totality*, which includes also the transcendent God, then the transcendent 'centre' of the world dependent on God is precisely this transcendent God who, it is true, is at the same time present to the world. But if one considers the world in itself, then its immanent centre is man, and it is the task and the responsibility of man to subject all the reality of the world to himself. Thus we read in the very first book of the Old Testament that man has the task of subjecting all the things of the world to himself, in order to rule over them (*Gen.* 1:26-8). And that means that man has to form not only the material world distinct from himself, but also himself and the lives of others in human society.

We know very well that not a few people are struck by a kind of fear when they look into the future. For it seems that in the near future man will have unsuspected possibilities—he will be able, for example, not only to transplant a human heart, but also to make far-reaching changes in the biological reality of man—with all the consequences that must follow for the human personality. The question is posed again—is it permitted to touch upon the reality of man? The answer must be, it is not only allowed, but it is even the duty of man constantly to make himself more a man, that is, always to develop himself further, and to bring into action the inner possibilities of the being that is called man. But here there is the difficulty of recognizing what kind of manipulation of man makes him more human. It would certainly be false to say—because God has created man as he finds himself to be in actuality, therefore this is the best manner of existence for men. For God has created man *complete with the possibility of his development,* and indeed of *self-development.* This is therefore man's duty even though we may have difficulties in recognizing which transformation of man represents a true human value.[2] But fundamentally we ought not to be afraid of touching upon the reality of man. On the contrary, this is our duty precisely because man, with these possibilities, is dependent upon God his Creator.

To regard man as the centre of this world, in so far as we see it in its autonomous immanence—that does not at all mean a subtle form of egoism. For it belongs to the essence

[2]To explain this difficulty we refer to Pius XII's discourse to the Italian Midwives in 1951. Speaking of the regulation of the natural fertility of married life, the Pope states that a similar intervention of human regulation is to be condemned if the intention is to exclude all conception from married life without sufficient reason (art. 35), but that such an intervention is permissible when sufficient reasons advise it (art. 36). However, he excludes as non-human all methods of regulation apart from abstinence and periodic continence. (This last assertion has just been reconfirmed by Paul VI in the recent encyclical *Humanae Vitae.*)

of a human being to open himself up to his neighbour. Thus the duty of forming the world and man as the lord of the world means in the first place the duty of responsibility for one's neighbour and ultimately the command to love him. It is highly interesting to discover that quite a few champions of a humanist ethic assume that responsibility for and love towards one's neighbour represent an absolute requirement of human morality, and that every other moral consideration is ultimately relative to this single absolute.

If a humanist morality does not take into consideration man's relationship to a transcendent God, that does not mean that a truly human morality, that is, a morality of man in so far as he is man, does not also include within itself the relationship of man to God, upon whom this world, in its relative autonomy, depends. Outside Christianity too, man, as such, has the possibility of discovering in the totality of his moral outlook the value and concept of religion and the relationship to God. In reality, then, the religious relationship to God belongs to the complete concept of a human morality, even though *in fact* not many people achieve this understanding.

A further brief reference should be made to another point, which can be established only with great difficulty in a human morality as such, at least so long as it prescinds from the reality of a transcendent Creator God. If one sees man as the centre of the world, as he is represented in the first book of holy Scripture, the question arises of whether the relinquishing of this world, the abstaining from it, and even a certain fleeing from the world, could be an element of human morality as such. But difficult though this question may be, it would seem nonetheless that man as such, even without the Christian revelation, even as an agnostic or an atheist, can attain from his own experience to a certain understanding about relinquishing the things of the world and abstaining from them. The following reasons might be suggested for this:

(*a*) Man, as such, is able to attain to the insight that love is the most important element in human morality, and at the same time he can learn from experience that love, that is absolute surrender to another, stands opposed to that self-centred egoism which is alive in every man. The agnostic and the atheist, too, can make this discovery. Thus a man begins to understand that precisely in order to attain his own self-realization, that is, love of his neighbour, he needs to acquire certain habits and to practise a certain asceticism, since otherwise he cannot overcome his egoism.

(*b*) Man, as such, discovers that he must reach a certain harmony within his own self. On the other hand, he discovers a deep egoism that obstructs this harmony within himself. When he makes this discovery, then he begins to see the meaning of what we call flight from the world or abstinence from the things of the world.

(*c*) It is plain that this becomes clearer as soon as a man attains to an explicit, categorical recognition of his transcendent God. For with the discovery of his own egoism he begins to understand also that it is precisely a certain flight from the world or a certain asceticism within it that *can* be a sign of belonging to God and of subjection to him. It should be noticed that the three motives cited are all based on man's experience of himself as egoist. For were it not for this inward inclination of man to egoism, there would be no reason for any kind of asceticism, whether as a sign of his own complete surrender to God, or in order to attain to an inner harmony within his own self, or in order to be able more truly to love his neighbour.

Human morality is thus a morality which can be recognized as such both by believing Christians and also by humanists. To be sure, it is another question whether Christians and humanists will really agree on every single question relating to human morality, but *basically* human morality is a morality that could be recognized and acknowledged by anyone.

II. CHRISTIAN MORALITY

When one comes to speak of Christian morality as Christian, there is reason to fear that some people will at once be disappointed. The reason for this fear lies in the fact that not many Christians have a really adequate idea of the relation between Christian and human morality. Presumably a good many of them, when they hear the phrase 'human morality', think at once of the morality of certain humanists, perhaps of the somewhat low moral standard of certain humanists. Anyone who wants to institute a comparison between the human morality that has been discussed, and Christian morality as Christian, must make this comparison between the ideal of Christian morality and the ideal of a truly human morality. If one poses the comparison in this way, it will become clear that Christian morality is *in essence* a true human morality.

In fact the first thing that should be said here about Christian morality is this, that it is a human morality, in the best sense of the word; in other words, that the moral conduct of the Christian must essentially be human conduct. It will perhaps be feared by some that this assertion is not entirely covered by the sayings of the evangelists, or of St Paul, or of Catholic tradition? Does not the Lord say to us that we would 'not be of this world' (*John* 15:19 and 17:16)? But 'to be of the world' means to live in this sinful world after the manner of sinners. According to the Lord (*John* 17:18), we have to live in this world—with man at its centre; to live therefore in human morality with its basic principle the love of neighbour. In other words, truly human conduct is an essential element of Christian morality. The apostle of the nations gives the same teaching. He warns Christians to live honourably because the heathens and the Jews also know well what is humanly dishonourable and what is morally good (*Rom.* 1–3). He insists that Christians are not to live dishonourably because, if their conduct is not truly human, the reputation of Christianity will suffer in the non-Christian world which, without being Christian, does indeed also know how to distinguish between what is honourable and what is not (*Rom.* 12:17; 1 *Cor.* 10:32; 1 *Thess.* 4:12). Paul therefore presupposes that the moral conduct of Christians must be the same as that of other men. And he adds that the Christians and the others, that is, heathens and Jews, will be judged by God according to the same works. This, however, means that the commands of moral conduct are the same for the one as for the other (*Rom.* 2:1; 2:6–11). And in fact, when Paul warns Christians to separate themselves from the men of this world, he in no way insists that the conduct of Christians should be different from that of good non-Christians, but much more that their conduct should be different from that of sinners, that is to say, from the conduct of men who do not live according to a true human morality. So far as the tradition of Catholic theology is concerned, one reference to Thomas Aquinas will suffice. The great teacher of the Middle Ages declares explicitly that no new moral directives are given by Jesus Christ beyond those dictated by human virtue.[3]

If this is so, then there arises for Christians and non-Christians the same epistemological problem, that is, to recognize what really is in fact human and what is not, what is or is not a human value, what is or is not honourable for a man. This question is the same for non-Christians and Christians, the criteria for distinguishing between good and bad, honourable and dishonourable, are the same for them as for us. Is adultery truly human or not? Is a lie a truly human proceeding or not? Are adultery and lying permissible or not for a man who wants to be human in the full sense? This question is the same for Christians and non-Christians. So it remains that the principles and

[3] St Thomas, *S. theol.*, 1–11, q. 108, a. 2.

I

commands of moral conduct are the same for a truly human
morality as for Christian morality.[4]

Beyond doubt, questions arise here. It will be asked, is love
of neighbour the new commandment of Christ or is it not?
Or at the least the commandment to love one's enemies?
Is it specifically Christian to help the needy, to care for the
incurably sick, to divert the riches of the developed nations
to the development of the underdeveloped, or is it a commandment of human morality? One can find even in some
books of Catholic ethics and morality the idea that human
morality (also termed the morality of the natural moral law)
knows only the virtue of justice, but not that of love, this last
being solely a Christian virtue. To this it can be answered—
were that so, then those who do not know or acknowledge
Christ would be permitted to leave unregarded their
neighbour, the sick, the needy, the underdeveloped countries,
indeed they would be permitted to hate their enemies and,
consequently, to practise the methods of hatred, violence, and

---

[4]So it is a matter of the *content* of Christian morality, i.e. of a morality that is
truly Christian. This must be watched, for there is no guarantee that morality
presented as 'Christian' or preached in the Christian communion is above
correction and infallible in all its elements. A separate question from that of the
'Christian' or 'human' content of Christian morality is how in the Christian
communion one arrives at a knowledge of this content, at least in so far as
this is presented as purely 'human' and not sustained by the revealed word.
A point here is that neither the individual Christian nor the holder of office
can come to a knowledge of the moral truth by private revelation, no matter
how constituted. The context of Christian revelation can indeed indicate to the
faithful, to the Christian communion, a direction in which they will find it
easier to arrive at the knowledge of—human—morality under individual
aspects. For this reason and because of the constant help of the holy Spirit—
even if this does not exactly guarantee the truth in every individual question—
the Christian communion, the Church in its moral comprehension, is itself
a 'place' in which the presence of a true awareness of 'Christian' and 'human'
morality is to be presumed on principle. With regard to this moral consciousness
of the Christian communion what matters, in so far as it doesn't stem from the
revealed word, is that (1) the content of this morality is 'human', not distinctively
Christian, (2) the moral consciousness of the communion derives knowledgewise
from 'human' understanding, (3) in the attempt to come to an understanding
of 'human' morality, the believer bears in mind the moral consciousness of the
Christian communion on certain questions, allowing for the theological worth
of its interpretations.

so on. If one reflects on this it should be clear that showing love for one's neighbour in these ways is not specifically Christian in the sense that it does not belong to a human morality as such. The best theoreticians of humanist morality themselves tell us that to be truly human, justice is not enough. What is demanded above all is love of neighbour —indeed, love of neighbour is *the* absolute value of every human morality.

There now remains, however, this question: if Christian conduct is substantially identical with human conduct as such, in what sense can we speak of a specifically Christian morality? Can one point out, in Christian morality and Christian moral conduct, what is specifically Christian? Yes, of course one can point to the distinctive element of a Christian morality, and it is clear that it is the *decisive* element of Christian morality. This distinctive element of Christian morality is that specific *Christian intentionality* which transcends and fulfils all human moral values. How should this Christian intention be understood?

I ask: what exactly am I doing when I perform a good moral act? Am I doing nothing other than accomplishing this single moral act? Am I doing nothing more? Do I not also, beyond and through this single act, realize my own human personality—and this indeed with reference to an Absolute? But if this is so—and it is so—then this self-realization in relation to an Absolute is the decisive element in morality: for the single act as such is then really nothing other than an expression of this personal relation to the Absolute. It is true that in our particular moral acts we do not think constantly and reflexively of the Absolute and our relation to it. Nonetheless a man is aware, even without explicit reflection, that in his good or evil deeds he realizes not only the deeds themselves, but also his own self, and himself in relation to the Absolute. Indeed it is precisely thus that the individual act is in reality a moral act. There is, therefore, a certain intentionality which transcends and fulfils the individual moral act, even when the consciousness of this intentionality is not reflected on and made explicit in every action.

To be sure, the intentionality so far described is not typically and specifically Christian. The Christian does not relate himself only to God as the Absolute and the Creator. He relates himself to God as Father, to God who in Christ gave us, in his fatherly love, the gift of his own Son. The Christian relates himself to a God who became incarnate in Christ in order to be our brother and saviour. The Christian has become a son of God in the spirit of Christ, which is given to him, and thus relates himself with Christ as son to the Father of the salvation which he has attained in Christ. The Christian is aware of this Christian reality in his moral dealings. And so he fulfils and makes specific his deep-seated intentionality as a moral action and relates it—as faith and hope and love—to the Father of our salvation in Jesus Christ. This Christian intentionality is what makes the moral behaviour of the Christian truly and specifically Christian, at every moment and in every aspect, even when it appears at first to be simply conduct conforming to human morality. In other words, there is nothing in the moral life and conduct of the Christian that is not filled with this Christian intentionality and consequently also the expression and manifestation of this Christian intentionality—that is, of the personal, conscious and freely-willed relation to the Father of Jesus Christ.

It is important to observe that this Christian intentionality is present in us not only when we think explicitly about our personal relation to Christ and through him to the heavenly Father. Rather is it known to us and also willed by us without explicit and systematic reflection upon it. Indeed this intentionality is present even to the sinner, though in a negative form. Through his sinful deed freely willed (at least in mortal sin), the sinner refuses to accept Christ and the relation to the Father of Jesus Christ. This is the Christian meaning of sin: the person who sins is not only unjust, disobedient, disloyal, etc. He is, rather, setting himself up in opposition to God as the Absolute and the Creator, and is consciously withholding himself (even if not in explicit reflection) from Christ the Lord and his Father in heaven.

In order fully to understand the essence of Christian morality it is not enough to consider the two elements already depicted, that is, human morality and the transcendental Christian intentionality that fulfils conduct conforming to human morality. There is yet a third element to be considered. In faith, the Christian recognizes and acknowledges certain realities which he alone can recognize and acknowledge. These realities are: the person of Christ, the holy Spirit working in us, the message of salvation—together with a Christian anthropology—the Church, the Christian community, the hierarchy, the sacraments, the teaching authority, etc.

As every man has to realize the given facts of his life and his own self in relation to these given facts, so the Christian must also realize in his life those realities and given facts that he recognizes and acknowledges in faith. It might perhaps be thought by some that all this, that is, the realizing of our relation to Christ, to the Church, to the Christian community, and so on, is not morality in the real sense, but much more religious practice. Whoever thinks like that must not forget, however, that religious life as such is also part of moral life. Besides, the recognition and acceptance (in faith) of Christian reality, not only makes possible the *transcendental* Christian intention, which has already been discussed, but also the concrete, *specific* motivation. Think for example of St Paul: in order to keep Christians free from the sin of fornication or of lying, he does not refer to human or to philosophical considerations (1 *Cor.* 6:12–20; *Eph.* 4:25). Rather he invokes the special dignity of the body of the Christian and the mutual relationship of Christians in a Christian community. Furthermore, anyone who knows the anthropology of the Christian message and follows in freedom the person of Christ crucified and risen, will, as Thomas

Aquinas showed, find special motives for putting into practice the virtue of moderation and a corresponding asceticism in earthly life.[5] If celibacy can be understood humanly as a rational freeing of oneself for an ideal commitment within the human community, then the ideal of Christian virginity can only be understood and accepted by someone who conceives the human situation in accordance with a complete Christian anthropology. If Christians readily help the poor, attend to social justice and devote themselves to the development of the less developed peoples they are practising not only a praiseworthy philanthropy but true Christian and theological charity. To speak more generally, the whole richness of Christian reality, which a man recognizes and accepts in faith, will have a continuing and living influence on his entire moral life, so long as his faith lives. To repeat: living Christian faith not only makes possible *transcendental,* supernatural and Christian intention, but it also ensures that the *specific,* religious and moral life is continually and most powerfully determined and influenced by all the variety of elements which make up the treasure of Christian reality.

There remains, perhaps, a special problem. It is certain that there also belongs to Christian reality, and that in a quite fundamental way, the *cross of Christ,* that is, total self-giving to others and their salvation. Does one not have to say that this element of Christian reality, the cross, is diametrically opposed to man as such and to human morality? But if that were really so, the Christian principle of the cross would exclude the substantial identification that we have made between human and Christian morality. Let us explore the question further. That upon which our salvation depends is in reality the cross of Christ, but it is well to say, not the cross as cross, as denial of life, as destruction, as sacrifice, but much rather as total self-giving which, to be sure, in the human world of sin and egoism, becomes

[5]St Thomas, *De Virtutibus,* a. 10 ad 8: cf. *S. theol.,* 1–11, q. 63, a. 4c.

sacrifice and cross. The love of neighbour, however, that total self-giving love, is indeed diametrically opposed to the *egoistic tendency of 'fallen man'*, but not to the true nature of *man as such* and his morality, that is, human morality. On the contrary it is, as already indicated, the deepest impulse of a truly human morality. If egoistic fallen man, when he follows Christ, perceives in himself an inclination contrary to the love of neighbour and its corresponding total self-giving, so that for him love and self-giving become cross and sacrifice, then this originates not in human nature as such, but rather in the egoistic being of fallen man. As, therefore, love of neighbour is not opposed to a truly human morality, but rather represents its central value, so also sacrifice and the cross, into which true love is transformed in egoistic man, do not in reality stand in opposition to a human morality but in close connection with it, given the 'situation of the Fall'. On the other hand it remains true that without the recognition and acknowledgement of Christian reality, without the special enlightenment and strength that come from it, man will not so easily grasp that sacrifice and cross are in accord with a truly human morality, and why this is so.

This is how we can understand better the Lord's Sermon on the Mount (*Matt.* 5–7). It is impossible to mention here all the interpretations which this discourse has had, but it seems to me that its Christian demands pertain to us precisely as men who are living already in the eschatological age, even if these last times have had as yet only their beginning. In this state of ours, of being men who are 'fallen' but already redeemed in Christ, the sole absolute is God and—from the moral point of view—self-giving love. This carries through to their 'rigorous' consequences the things Christ points out by means of examples in his discourse. Man feels Christ's demands to be 'rigorous' to the extent that he is 'fallen', that is, egoistic; and the demands are only made possible by the presence of Christ's grace. Here again we see that the opposition pointed out by the Lord's discourse lies precisely between the egoism of 'fallen'

man and the demand of love which becomes a cross to man
to the extent that he is egoistic, namely 'fallen', but not to
man as such. And it is the grace of the Redeemer which
leads to the overcoming of man's egoism and not man and
human morality as such. I would be inclined to put it like
this: what Christ preaches in the Sermon on the Mount as
something new is not really a new—Christlike as distinct
from simply human—morality, but a new mankind van-
quishing the 'old mankind of the Fall'. The genuine morality
of mankind is of value in that kingdom of God announced
and brought to us by Christ; and it is truly practised by the
members of God's kingdom in its spirit of openness which
overcomes an egoistical self-centred inclination. There is no
point in explaining here the meaning of the individual
requirements made by the Sermon on the Mount. Suffice it
to note that the Lord speaks using parables and images and
that for this reason every purely *literal* interpretation is
insufficient. In the Lord's own life there were occasions when
he acted in a way contrary to the literal meaning of the
words of his discourse.

A further question is quite often raised in connection with
our idea of the relation between human and Christian
morality, and this must also be considered here. Does there
not exist between human and Christian morality the
fundamental difference of an essentialist, static and apersonal
morality on the one side and a dynamic, interpersonal
morality of vocation on the other? This difference can be
represented in the following way: human morality concerns
the realization of man's being. To be a man is a given and
known reality. It is man's moral duty to live this reality.
Christian morality, on the contrary, desires the openness of
men to the call of God the Saviour, a call that cannot be
reckoned with in advance, because it is a call of salvation.
This divine call of salvation ultimately even determines the
concrete relationship of the Christian to his neighbour. That
is why we say that human morality and Christian morality
are diametrically opposed. The same opposition is also

expressed in another formulation. It is said that human morality relates to the temporal reality of man in the sense of *chronos,* that is, the sense of time which repeats itself in identical form and can therefore be calculated, whereas Christian morality relates to human temporality in the sense of *kairos,* that is, the sense of the qualitative time of the moment which is not calculable, because it is determined by what leads us to salvation. However, it may be asked, in reply to this consideration, whether that openness of man towards the incalculable God, a dynamic and interpersonal openness therefore, does not belong to the *essence of man* in his relation to God? If that were not so, how could a man who was not open, not dynamic, not interpersonal, understand the divine revelation of the open, dynamic and interpersonal man? Besides, if God can, and in fact does, call his creature in an unforeseeable way, then a man cannot indeed, it is true, establish or consider *a priori* in what way God will call him but equally he cannot, on the other hand, be called by God other than as man, and thus not in contradiction to the structural principles of man's morality, that is, of a human morality. So 'Christian newness'—to give it for once this name—has to be explained in another way: 1. 'Fallen man' does not come so easily to clear and explicit recognition of the true connection between God and man as this is and should be according to his true nature. Here a Christian anthropology offers to man great help on the way to true self-knowledge. 2. God's call is in fact a call of salvation, and the manner in which this saving call occurs, in the concrete, in man's daily life can be known solely from the message that only the Christian knows, through his faith. This double aspect (1 and 2) belongs unambiguously to the third element of the analysis of Christian morality given above—but not to its basic character as an open, dynamic and interpersonal morality.

The attempt at an analysis of Christian morality leads us to the discovery of a threefold substance: firstly, the human element, that is, human morality; secondly, the distinctive element, that is, the transcendental, specifically Christian intentionality; and thirdly, the acceptance and putting into practice of the Christian realities of our faith in so far as these determine our religious life, typically Christian motivations, and even moral conduct. This attempt at an analysis begins with that element which at first glance seems to be the most basic for us men, that is, human morality as such.

This procedure is justified, though it can rightly be considered somewhat abstract. There is another way, less abstract and closer to actuality, and in this sense more true: the Christian who truly believes and whose faith is a living faith which determines his life in the concrete, knows himself as saved in Christ, baptized in Christ, called in Christ, and called above all to give himself to the Father of Christ in the spirit of a son of God. Accordingly he tries to live before the Father in true self-surrender, as a man saved, baptized, and called. This is the most important and most basic element of Christian morality. It fills and defines the whole Christian life. But this Christian intentionality must be lived out in the concrete, that is, daily put into practice and expressed in concrete, particular and specific acts and tendencies. The man of faith must live his faith and his love, he must express them, put them into practice concretely. And that, indeed, *first* by a truly human life among the men of this world, which means, however, according to a truly human morality, as Paul represents it. And *then* by the integration of the whole of Christian reality, as it can be understood by faith, into the Christian's life of human morality. Or, better, the believing Christian finds that he must live in Christian love by realizing the whole reality of his Christianity in all the acts of his life, a reality to which belong also his human nature together with the whole human morality of a Christian.

If one looks at the problem like this, that is less abstractly and in a much more concrete and realistic way, it is clear that what is human, and human morality in itself, constitute a most deeply Christian reality—in the sense that they do not exist in a pure and distilled state but are always already integrated and filled with a specifically Christian intentionality and are therefore the expression of this intentionality, and are always open to all the elements of Christian faith. When one speaks of *human* morality as such, one is really speaking already of Christian morality, even if under a particular aspect, its human aspect. It remains true that the human aspect of Christian morality can itself be discovered and understood by the human spirit, independently of the fact of whether people are Christians or not. As has already been demonstrated above, the criteria by which we must determine which kind of human conduct is truly human, that is, in accordance with right reason, are in themselves the same for all men. To be sure, it is true that the revelation of Christ and consequently also holy Scripture and Christian tradition are necessary to come to the recognition of the *totality* of Christian reality and morals. It is also true that this revelation can be important and sometimes morally necessary, so that all men can come to a recognition of the principles of a human morality and that indeed with adequate certainty and without error. But it is just as true that the human element of Christian morality *in itself*, that is human morality, is not inaccessible to recognition by the human mind. Besides, for the greater part of the moral norms and concrete solutions of a human morality there is no special and specific statement of revelation at all.

III. CHRISTIAN MORALITY AND HUMANIST MORALITY

It is apparent from the foregoing reflections on the essence of a human morality as such and the essence of Christian morality as Christian, and on their mutual relation, that it is possible and necessary to make a comparison between Christian morality and humanist-secularist morality. It is clear from the start that a *humanist* morality is not simply the same as a *human* morality, and that on the other hand a humanist morality cannot contain the entire richness of Christian morality. What are the common elements and what the differences in humanist as compared with Christian morality? An answer to this question can be made possible by again considering the three elements in Christian morality distinguished above:

1. So far as Christian morality's own 'human morality' is concerned, this is not in itself closed to the humanist, inasmuch as it is only a question of finding out what kind of human behaviour is truly human and in accordance with right reason. There remains only the epistemological difficulty of discovering what is in reality the content of a human morality. But this question confronts not only the humanist, but also the Christian, in the same way.

2. The most important element of Christian morality, as has been shown, is the transcendental, specifically Christian intentionality. A difficult theological question arises here, that of whether the humanist, too, can and must live this element. A positive answer, that is that the non-believing humanist is also capable of this transcendental Christian intentionality cannot, it seems, be simply ruled out, especially since the Second Vatican Council expressed itself concerning the call of non-Christians to salvation in Christ.[6] This answer would mean that the good non-Christian also fulfils his practice of human morality with an intentionality that is in a real sense Christian, and that the non-Christian sinner offends not only against the order of human morality, and not only against the God of creation, but also against the Father of Jesus Christ and the Christian vocation. How is one to understand this? On the one hand, if God has prepared salvation for all men, then—it would seem—the gift and grace of a personal call in Christ must also be there for all men as individuals. On the other hand an adult cannot be compelled to salvation in Christ; he has rather

---

[6]2nd Vatican Council: *Lumen Gentium* art. 8 and 16: *Ad Gentes* art. 3: *Gaudium et Spes* art. 22.

to accept the gift of grace in freedom, that is, he must make a personal response to his call in Christ. It is, however, obvious that he cannot make this response if he is not personally aware of his call in Christ. There remains only the question of how one can explain the Christian vocation and one's personal experience of it to a man who does not know or accept Christ. In order to reach a solution to this problem it is well to consider how a *Christian* carries over his Christian intentionality into the practice of human morality. This Christian intentionality is without doubt a conscious intentionality, even though it is not carried out in a formal, reflexive and conceptual consciousness. In addition it is good to bring it home to oneself that grace is effective precisely in that innermost region where a person, as such, realizes his own self in relation to the Absolute. Precisely in that innermost region where he is present to himself, as Thomas Aquinas says,[7] where he is conscious of himself and not only of his act, there in that true yet not reflexive consciousness comes God's call, the call of Christ, the Christian vocation. In this innermost region, at this centre of the person, the non-Christian, too, can experience the call of Christ in genuine even if not in reflexive and specific consciousness. And therefore he can also, precisely in this central region, accept or reject the Christian vocation in genuine, even if not reflexive consciousness and freedom. But the non-Christian, in accepting or rejecting the Christian vocation and with it his salvation, puts into his realization or non-realization of human morality a Christian or anti-Christian intentionality. Thus the humanist also possesses not only the capacity for human conduct but he has in addition, and much more, the capacity to charge this human conduct with a Christian intentionality in a real sense, that is, the intentionality of a son of God in relation to the Father of Jesus Christ. It is true that only the Christian is able to reflect upon this Christian intentionality, while the non-Christian, on the contrary, is not.

[7] St Thomas, *Contra Gentes* IV, 11: *S. theol.* 1, q. 87, a. 1.

3. We come now to the third element in our analysis of
Christian morality. The non-Christian does not have
Christian faith. In his specific consciousness there does not
exist the reality of the person of Jesus Christ, of salvation, the
gospel, the Church, the sacraments, the community of the
Christian peoples, and so on. And for him the cross and the
resurrection as realities of saving significance do not exist
either. Therefore all these Christian realities can have no
specific influence on his motivation and on the practice of
his moral life.

IV.   LOVE AS THE HIGHEST MORAL VALUE

It might be of use to consider expressly the most important
value of a human morality, as accepted by Christians and
humanists alike—love.

Christian morality regards love as the highest moral value.
So much so that all the moral virtues are simply not capable
of making a man morally good unless they are the expression
of love. Love is to be understood as the self-giving of the
Christian after the manner of Christ's love for the Father,
and as a participation in this love. Holy Scripture explains
to us that love of neighbour is in a certain sense identical
with love of God, that is, that self-giving love is essentially
love of God.

It is therefore very interesting to see that many humanists
also classify love as *the* moral value, or even regard it as the
only moral value. To be sure, it must be noted that these
humanists are speaking only of love of neighbour, not of love
of God. But this love of neighbour they conceive as a non-
egoistic attitude towards their neighbour, and ultimately as
a non-egoistic gift of their own self. Some humanists speak in
this sense because they have a special sensitivity to the value
of the human person, or to the freedom that is ultimately
identical with the person, or to the fundamental equality of
all men. This attitude is also to be found among people who

have no religious understanding of man. Other humanists base their view concerning the fundamental value of love of neighbour on the person of Christ—thereby considering Christ less as the source of salvation and much more as the outstanding example of a lofty and truly human morality. Clearly, in this case they accept Christ in a more or less fideist manner, without being clear, in the last analysis, about his real nature.

The fact that not only Christians but also the best among the humanists insist upon the special value of love (of neighbour) is not only extremely interesting, but is also of the utmost importance. It is precisely in interpersonal relationships, and ultimately in love, that man, as such, discovers an absolute. So it seems that man always has a certain experience of his contingency, of not being absolute, of being conditioned—even if he does not reflect on this experience of his and does not try to clarify its implications, or perhaps even explicitly denies these implications or even the experience itself. This human experience is in fact a certain experience of the Absolute and of an absolute moral law. But what is it that is meant by 'experience of the Absolute' and 'transcendental relation to the Absolute', if not the duty of total submission, total surrender therefore of one's own self, which is ultimately love? This does not mean that man can only experience this transcendental relation to the Absolute in explicit experience of the duty of love of neighbour. But it is still interesting and highly significant to discover that the best among today's humanists regard precisely this, the proper relationship to one's neighbour, love, as in a real sense an *absolute* duty, and even indeed as the *sole* absolute moral value. They believe that in the last analysis moral value cannot be understood other than as interpersonal value. It is clear that they conceive the human person as essentially related to others. For this very reason they discover more easily and fully in the experience of their neighbour, of the human person, the idea of an Absolute and of an absolute obligation. One can understand this better if one takes into account that only the proper relationship to others, that is, love, can lead to free personal dependence and the free gift of one's own self, that is, of the person as such. The Absolute demands the person, demands love. Where the category of personal relations is not found within the concept of the Absolute, this concept lacks its true fullness and lacks life.

The problem now arises of how the Absolute, as experienced, should be understood. What is the Absolute? Many do not succeed in understanding the Absolute as that reality which is called God. It is significant nonetheless that man seeks to conceive the Absolute and absolute moral value in terms of interpersonal relationships, of self-giving, of love. Or, to put it differently: the person of another and relationship to him are more able to make comprehensible the category of the Absolute. This fact also enables us more easily to make acceptable the idea that every man, in a perception of the Absolute, has a true experience of *God*, even though in an unreflexive and non-specific manner. Precisely in the person of another, a man experiences, even if without specific reflection, the true Absolute, which is ultimately a *personal* reality. This privileged element in human morality, love as the highest and absolute value, as it is accepted by the best humanist morality, could well be the starting point for a further reflection that could lead to an understanding of the Absolute that was deeper and in a true sense personal, an understanding that would go beyond the humanist understanding of what is human, to reach a religious understanding. Thus love of neighbour would show itself to be ultimately a form of love of God.

Could the absolute value of love of neighbour also perhaps be the starting point—in the field of human morality—from which to come, possibly, to Christ? This is a theological question in the strict sense. What happens within a man and in his life when he really attains to love of neighbour? Theologically it seems that one must say that egoistic 'fallen man' will not arrive at true self-giving to others, at true love, except through the grace of the Saviour. To love means to give oneself—so the egoist cannot, by his own efforts, attain love. If, therefore, a man, even a humanist, loves in this manner, then his love is a sign that the grace of Christ is present and active in him. More, this grace is not only present and in some way effective in him, it is actually overcoming egoism. But that means the man himself is consciously and freely accepting the grace of Christ, the grace that effects love and the giving of self, even though without specific reflection. In other words, the man who loves his neighbour, that is, who truly gives himself, in fact freely accepts in love that same Christ whom he perhaps does not know or does not accept specifically, but whose call to give oneself, following his example, to the Father and to one's brothers, the man understands in a non-specific manner.

V. THE DIALOGUE WITH THE HUMANIST

We have already referred briefly to the possible dialogue between humanist and Christian. One cannot avoid the question of dialogue if one grasps the relationship between Christian and humanist morality as it has been described above.

It is clear that the first point at issue in a dialogue with the humanist concerns the field of human morality as such. To arrive at a truly human morality the Christian, as has been said above, requires the same criteria and the same epistemology as the humanist. Whether in fact Christians and humanists have already adequately worked out for themselves this epistemology and these criteria is another matter. The various discussions among Christians, as among humanists, show unmistakably that men are still in the process of understanding moral truth better and more correctly.

While Christians and non-Christians agree upon a number of points of human morality, this agreement is lacking on

K

other points. But this lack of agreement is found not only between Christians and humanists but also between Catholic and non-Catholic Christians, and even among Catholics themselves. One should not be surprised at this, for moral questions are not solved by logical and obvious deductions from concrete human reality. Moral 'solutions' are much more an 'understanding' of the kind of human behaviour that really corresponds to the being of man in its concrete realization. That is why it is not possible for me to 'demonstrate' to another, in the true sense, moral truth. The only thing I can do is to explain to the other and describe to him how I see and understand the matter, and in this way he will perhaps also begin to 'understand' it as I do. But who knows, perhaps we shall never arrive at the same understanding.

There are, however, also special difficulties for the dialogue between Christians and humanists.

It has already been pointed out that one of these difficulties is the question of abstinence, of non-use, of a certain flight from the world to the cross. Even if this aspect of Christian morality is not simply in opposition to human morality, there are still special difficulties for the humanist who represents a purely secular, self-contained morality, in arriving at the same considerations as the Christian, who accepts the reality of the person of Christ, his message of salvation and the Christian anthropology.

The most powerful obstacle to a full and true understanding of human morality is human egoism, the situation of man 'after the Fall'. The humanist, too, is a man 'after the Fall'. But as a non-believer he, unlike the Christian, has not been made explicitly aware of his situation and therefore he will overlook more easily than the Christian the way in which understanding of moral values can be dependent upon human egoism.

Certainly the Christian has many aids to the understanding of the truth of human morality from the whole context of revelation. He is made more easily receptive to true moral values by this context, and is perhaps also able to discover them more surely. Above all, there should not be forgotten here the meaning of the experience of the Christian community, which indeed lives always in the context of revelation.

On the other hand we now know very well that in the moral teaching of Christians there are also found non-Christian influences, and even influences that are not in the true sense human—one may think for example of certain influences of the Gnostics and of the *Stoa*. Thus it is by no means out of the question that on certain points of human morality some forms of humanism do not—or do no longer—display such influences inasmuch as they are able much more easily to free themselves from certain of these influences than a community bound by tradition. Thus Christians or the Christian community do not in every case hold an absolutely and exclusively privileged position so far as possession of the various values of human morality is concerned. So it is perfectly possible that dialogue with others, honourable common work, may prove a valuable help towards a fuller understanding of man and of human and moral behaviour. This cannot be ruled out even though the Christian, unlike the humanist, possesses advantages founded on the framework of the Christian revelation.

Dialogue concerning the religious implications of a human morality may be less easily possible. One cannot unmistakably and effectively 'demonstrate' to another the true interpretation of the Absolute which is implicit in a human morality and is also accepted in various forms by a serious humanism. The most important and perhaps the only thing that can be done in this respect is perhaps this: to help the other person to understand and respond, more deeply and intensely, to the absolute value of human morality. From this point there might perhaps take root in him one day a sense of the real life and morality of the Christian *as such*—if these are simply and honestly set out (not 'demonstrated'), as Christians understand them.

The conclusion of this consideration on the essence of

Christian morality and its relation to human, and humanist morality is as follows: in the dialogue with the humanists concerning moral questions it is of the utmost importance to establish co-operation in the search for the values of a human morality and in the deepening of our understanding of it. For this human morality will enable the good humanist, too, to live with truly religious and indeed, in a real sense, with Christian intentionality, even though not in a specific manner, and this is of the utmost importance. Whether the true and consistent humanist will in this way also arrive at an *explicitly* religious or even Christian understanding and with it at the fullness of Christian morality is another question.

VI. *Excursus:* HUMAN MORALITY AS NATURAL LAW
MORALITY

Human morality means natural law morality. Though leaving aside numerous problems of the doctrine of the natural moral law, the reflections on 'Human Morality' in Section I, including note 2, suggest that further consideration of the subject would be desirable; especially since so many have meanwhile taken up positions on that concept of natural law which underlies the encyclical 'Humanae Vitae'. In our reflections we shall make use of a twofold definition. When the apostle Paul speaks in Romans 2 about the reality which is nowadays called the natural moral law, he calls it a law 'engraved on their hearts' (2:15). Even today this definition can be met with. But many moral theologians prefer a different terminology and speak of a law 'engraved in nature'. Both terminologies, of course, express the same reality of the natural moral law. Both terminologies, likewise, can be correctly understood and both are therefore open to a similar interpretation. It does not follow that they are in fact always used in the same sense. The formulation, however, of natural moral law as 'law engraved in nature' is often understood in a sense which many people believe to be precisely that of the encyclical. Without wanting to analyse the encyclical's concept of natural law as such, it can be shown that two different ways of understanding the natural moral law underlie these two terminologies. This twofold understanding is, of course, important for the problems with which the encyclical deals.

'Engraved in nature'

To highlight the danger of a wrong interpretation of the above formula we need only refer to one question—a question which is seldom put in exactly this way, but which quite often finds a reply implicit in a certain interpretation of the natural moral law. The question is this: when God created man and his world did he also create a moral law—the natural law? There is no doubt that the natural moral law is often understood as an affirmative answer to this question. Quite often it is expressly so defined. In this decidedly inaccurate, if not erroneous, view the natural moral law is seen as 'created' by God; the Creator imposes the natural moral law on his creature, man. If this description of the phenomenon is deliberately somewhat strong and one-sided —with a view to letting the problem be seen quite clearly—it cannot, however, be easily denied that the concept described here often bears an unequivocal voluntarist and positivist stamp—a stamp which is basically at variance with the true concept of the natural moral law. For God's earthly creations are man and his world—and nothing else. But this man created by God is a being with body and soul. As such he is capable of discovering and comprehending himself, his being, his possibilities, his world and the meaning of this whole reality—mankind and his world—and of progressing with these discoveries and deepening this understanding. It is possible for man to discover the potential shape of his life, of man's communal existence and of the human formation of the world. If he wants to live and act in a human way he has nothing further to do but draw up a plan of his acts and his life. He will always have to beware lest any particular way of acting and living is not 'really human', i.e. does not conform to the existence of the human person in the given reality which is concrete, contingent and historical. Inasmuch as he does this correctly he is 'discovering' or 'recognizing' natural moral law.

The medieval Scholastics preferred to speak of the 'recta ratio'—not simply the 'ratio' (in its correct *or* incorrect usage)—rather than of the natural moral law. When we refer to 'man' and his reason, it is understood that individual man does not *in fact* exist as an island, finding out in isolation the potential shape of truly human conduct, but that this knowledge, this 'recta ratio' is achieved by mankind in its communal life and actions. So God did not create 'man' and superimpose on him the 'will of God' as natural law; God's will has just one end: that *man should be*—which at the same time implies that *he should be human*.

The natural moral law is therefore 'engraved in the nature of man' in the sense that man himself discovers and recognizes in the correct realization of his corporo-spiritual being the way of living and conduct which corresponds to this person in his concrete manhood. But the 'engraved in nature' aspect of the moral law is not understood by everybody in this way. Many theologians do not take the concept of 'nature' to be basically the body and soul reality of man in which—as a whole and as a unity—the natural moral law is engraved in the way we have explained. Rather they have been saying lately that the natural moral law is 'engraved', and consequently can be 'read', not primarily in the totality of man, but rather in components of this human reality, e.g. in his biological nature or his biological-physiological-psychological-sexual nature. It is expressly stated that God has incorporated and thus made clear 'his will' for the conduct of mankind in the biological make-up of man. Again this interpretation of the natural moral law is really a voluntarist and positivist one: for the will of his Creator is communicated to man as a totality (a being of body and soul) through the actual shaping of (for example) his biological sexuality as such. In this interpretation the relevant component, e.g. the biological nature, is regarded as a part of the human person, yet the personal comprehension of man in his totality is missing; biological nature itself is not understood in a personal sense.

What can be directly 'read' in man's biological nature is only the manner in which nature works spontaneously if man does not intervene, or also the possible results man can achieve if he wishes to make use of nature functioning in this manner. In other words, what man can read directly in physical nature as such is nothing more than *facts*—to which the *physical* laws of nature pertain. Thus, it is a physical law that rape may result in pregnancy, and that this consequence can be prevented by a premature suspension of ovulation. On the other hand, which use of these physical laws is morally justifiable cannot be discerned from physical nature as such. In order to discover the moral in the use of physical reality and physical laws an understanding is necessary of the meaning, the significance and the importance of the given physical nature in the totality of the human person as such. The norm of correct moral behaviour cannot simply be found in the fact of its conformity with physical nature as such, but rather in its conformity with the human person taken in his totality—not, therefore, without regard for the peculiarity of purely physical nature. Human freedom in a moral context is not simply subject to the physical laws as such. Rather they should be made use of by man as a person to proceed with the development of himself and his world along truly human, that is humanizing, lines, i.e. to set in motion that possibility of the development of mankind and his world which proceeds from God. Thus it is not the physical law that has to be considered as a moral law and invoked to regulate the free actions of mankind, but the 'recta ratio' which understands the *person* in the *totality* of his reality.

'Engraved on the heart'

There is no doubt that the idea of the moral order described as 'engraved in nature' is open to misunderstanding and that it has often been misunderstood in Christianity—principally on the strength of centuries-old interpretations. Then the Pauline formula of the law 'engraved on the heart' presents itself. Of course Paul as a Jewish Christian is here speaking of the Old Testament law; but he means that the heathen who has not received the law of the Old Testament is nonetheless able to become aware of that law; not indeed the law itself and as such, i.e. as revealed, but rather 'the works of the law'—its contents. In other words the morality of truly human existence, revealed to the Jews in the law of the Old Testament, is 'engraved on the heart' of the heathen, i.e. man, even when this law hasn't been revealed to him. What does it mean, then, to say that human morality is 'engraved on the heart'? Like nature, the heart is not a book which man can simply open and read; likewise it is not implied that man possesses an instilled or inborn knowledge. It is, therefore, simply impossible that the natural moral law should indicate not only a few general principles, but also man's correct behaviour in many and widely varying external and internal acts. The Pauline formula means rather that man, in knowing himself as man, can understand himself as a moral being too—at least fundamentally. He can know how to act and behave in such a way that his individual actions, his life and future, are or may be in accord with (concrete) human existence and so be worthy of man (or corresponding to man's dignity).

The question could of course be raised, how one may achieve this 'understanding' of the natural moral law as that 'engraved on the heart'. An entire book would have to be written on this question. But here a few remarks may suffice. First of all, the formula 'compatible with (concrete) human existence' requires a short explanation. This phrase has often been taken to mean that man 'deduces' the 'moral order' of his actions from his 'being', although perhaps without explicitly saying so. Of course the *correspondence* between the concrete state of man's being and his moral actions must be insisted upon. But we should not speak of *deducing* moral norms from man's being and his circumstances. Moral categories cannot be deduced from ontological categories. There is, however, a mental 'insight', 'understanding', 'intuition'—even if the understanding is not reflexive, or, better, the basis of the insight. The position is actually this; man, who has always known himself as a person and as a being with moral responsibilities and inclinations, strives to answer the moral query—which mode of action in its specific category corresponds to his moral orientation as already experienced (Thomas: 'appetitus rectus')?

Man can only answer this moral question when he has sufficient knowledge of his concrete being, i.e. his being as such (*a priori*) as well as of the total concrete reality of man (*a posteriori*)—and understands it in the fullness of its meaning—in the totality of the concrete man. Every man has an *a priori* awareness—after more or less reflection—of some of the essential elements of his being; of his contingency to, and total dependence on an absolute; his fundamental interpersonal individuality and the corresponding social orientation to others, but above all of his own personality, freedom and responsibility. This *a priori* knowledge does not of course suffice to arrive at concrete moral judgements beyond very general insights like sociability, love, responsibility and the like. Any more concrete judgement presupposes the experience and the understanding of concrete reality, with its latent possibilities, the physical, psychological, interpersonal, etc. consequences of certain behaviour in the realm of such concrete reality, the manifold of their possible significance in the totality of concrete human existence, the fact that certain realities and values are historically and sociologically conditioned and so forth. The real question is as follows: what sort of behaviour in a definite sphere of reality and taking everything into account is 'reasonable', 'human' (in the best and fullest sense of this word), 'creative of human values' (in a total sense and consequently not merely—for example—in the biological, psychological, physical sense) 'corresponds to the dignity of man's existence as a person'? In the past various attempts were made to establish criteria for the correct answers to the moral question: such as the suitability of a mode of action to the fostering of interpersonal and community relationships, the consequences of certain modes of action in the different spheres of human existence and association (of which man cannot have an *a priori* knowledge, but can know only through some experience), the demand that there be a possibility of true harmony between man's rights and duties, the various forms taken by behaviour-patterns in different groups and cultures and the success or failure of these in the formation of a truly worthy picture of man and of a healthy human community and in the further development of mankind in a way compatible with its dignity.

In the past it has been emphasized that in the case of a moral judgement upon an action the material content of the action should be considered. This observation is important in so far as one often gets the impression from contemporary writing that the material content of the action itself contributes nothing towards the judgement of its morality. Such a tendency in an ethic is absolutely opposed to that other extreme view which only takes into consideration the material content of the action as such in the formation of a moral judgement. If this second extreme is erroneous the first is equally so. A human person cannot give to each action the meaning that *suits him*. The meaning of the action and the moral judgement upon it also depend on its content and possible meaning for man whether in general or in its concrete limitations and make-up. The correct use of sex cannot be judged by the biological or psychological reality of sexuality alone, nor by man's personal existence alone, but only by the meaningfulness of the human person's self-realization through a definite type of behaviour in the sphere of biological and psychological sexuality. It has long been in question whether spontaneous fecundity can be directed or regulated in marriage. In other words, can the control of spontaneous fecundity be meaningful and in conformity with the total personal reality of man? Well before the Second Vatican Council, Pius XII gave an answer in the affirmative in his famous address to married couples in 1951. To the supplementary question of whether this controlling intervention by the human person may only be accomplished by partial or total abstinence, the Papal Commission of Pope Paul VI, established to deal with these questions, came forward with a different answer from that which the Pope himself finally gave in the encyclical *Humanae Vitae*. When the question arose some years ago whether it was morally permissible for a woman faced with the danger of rape to protect herself from unwanted consequences by the use of contraceptives (the 'pill'), some theologians regarded as very conservative replied in the affirmative, whereas others persisted in a different judgement; the discussion of this question has not yet led to a unanimous solution. In this and in many other questions where can we find the law 'engraved on the heart' and consequently the 'will of God'? They are not to be seen either as a fact or as a structure of behaviour as such. But they are equally not identifiable with the good intentions of man acting as a person. Only from the total meaningfulness of an action centred in the concrete total reality of the human person can the mode of action which is morally right be seen, grasped, 'read in the heart'. These few examples show that it is not always easy for man to interpret that law 'engraved on the heart' correctly, positively and without possibility of doubt. But these examples also show that the concept 'natural law'—'law engraved in nature'—'law engraved on the heart'—is by no means understood by all in the same way.

6 Moral Theology and Dogmatic Theology[1]

A moral theologian said recently that he wished it were possible to present moral theology, or at least fundamental morals, as a dogmatic tract. A dogmatic theologian, on the other hand, stated that the basic themes of moral theology should be reserved for dogmatic theology. Both positions share the awareness that moral theology, at least in its essentials, is one of the many possible dogmatic tracts. Both statements give evidence of the efforts being made to counteract the frequently lamented separation of the two disciplines that centuries ago formed one undivided discipline. Yet no one is dreaming of simply welding moral and dogmatic theology together again to make one single discipline. Even the specialization in different branches of knowledge that is necessary nowadays would prevent such a fusion. But specialization is not the only reason for maintaining the separation. In one sense there has always been a special discipline of moral theology different from what we nowadays would call dogmatic theology. In the days of the great theological summas, which presented dogmatic and moral theology as one whole, there were still 'practical' summas which were not only practical reference books but also text-books of practical moral theology. One thing is clear: whatever one's concept or definition of moral theology is, dogmatic theology, the systematic clarification of the deposit of the Christian faith, will always be of great importance to it. And so the purpose of this chapter is to

[1]Article 'Moraltheologie und Dogmatik', in *Gregorianum* (50) 1969.

deal with the relationship of moral to dogmatic theology. From the theoretical point of view they form a single discipline: that is the basic thesis. But in so far as they are for practical reasons treated as two special disciplines one can justifiably speak of the importance of dogmatic for moral theology.

The theme 'Moral Theology and Dogmatic Theology' will be treated from three different aspects: I. Moral theology as dogmatic theology: it will be shown that moral theology is theology in the same sense as dogmatic theology is, that theoretically moral and dogmatic theology form one single discipline. II. A moral dogmatic theology or a dogmatic moral theology? It will appear that basic themes of moral theology can be treated just as well under the heading of dogmatic theology. III. Two incomplete and complementary disciplines: I shall demonstrate the importance of these two disciplines for each other, given the division into two; here special attention will be paid to the importance of dogmatic for moral theology.[2]

[2]On the relationship between moral and dogmatic theology cf. P. Delhaye, 'Dogme et Moral' in *Problemi scelti di Teologia contemporanea*, Rome 1954, 27–39 (also in *Mél. Sc. Rel.*, 11, 1954, 49–62): K. Rahner, 'Dogmatik', in *Lex. f. Theol. und Kirche*, III², 446–8: J. Rief, 'Zum theologischen Charakter der Moraltheologie', in *Theologie im Wandel* (Festsch. . . . kath-theol. Fakultät der Univ. Tübingen), Munich 1967, 518–42.

K. Rahner writes in the article referred to: 'The nature of dogmatic theology can, to begin with, be described simply as follows: it is the theological science of dogma. In that capacity it will take as its object the whole of Christian revelation, and therefore those dogmas also which have a "moral" content. In the early days of the Church and in the Middle Ages the one theological science (even if not called "dogmatic theology") embraced both "theoretical" and "practical" dogmas, and in fact even today in its dogmatic anthropology it deals with all the essential themes of the theology of morality that derive immediately from the word of God (a supernatural goal, sinfulness, being in Christ, justification, the theological virtues, sacraments, etc.). Consequently even today it leaves to moral theology for the most part only the practical details of Christian behaviour in the application of the theological principles that dogmatic theology itself lays down in its examination of the essential structures of the Christian reality. The maxims of Christian behaviour follow from these structures. . . . And so in the relations between moral and dogmatic theology there can only be question of an absolutely extrinsic (though dangerous) and technical division of labour in a science which has a strict unity. Consequently,

1. MORAL THEOLOGY AS DOGMATIC THEOLOGY

Moral and dogmatic theology not only *can* be treated as the one Christian theology, dogmatic theology; they *have been* so treated. Dogmatic theology has in itself no compelling reason for refusing to handle that part of the deposit of faith that refers to the more practical side of Christian living. This is, however, true only on condition that the full theological depth of the concerns of moral theology be seen and appreciated. We will try different approaches to the theme 'Moral theology as dogmatic theology': 1. 'De fide et moribus', 2. Dogmatic theology as Christian anthropology: indicative and imperative, 3. Moral theology as 'developed' dogmatic theology, 4. The 'dogmatic' character and method of moral theology.

'De fide et moribus'

Theology and the magisterium regard themselves as competent in questions '*de fide et moribus*'.[3] Without investigating the time and place of origin of this formula we may take it that there is a certain parallel here to the distinction between dogmatic and moral theology. We can also assume that *mores* means not simply—or at least not exclusively—the content of the natural law of morals, but refers to moral

---

moral theology too belongs to the central core of that science of the faith that we now call dogmatic theology. Or, to put it another way, moral theology is the practical science for the evaluation and application of the insights gained by dogmatic theology into the supernatural aspects of morality. These insights it applies with the help of non-theological disciplines (psychology, ethics, etc.) and secular experience. Moral theology could also be regarded as a middle between these two possibilities. In any case it is not necessary from the theoretical point of view to restrict dogmatic theology to one part of the dogmas of Christianity.'

[3]Cf. M. Bévenot, ' "Faith and Morals" in the Council of Trent and Vatican I', *The Heythrop Journal* (3) 1962, 15–30; P. Fransen, "Geloefen zeden": notitie over een veelgebruikte formule', *Tijdschrift V, Theol.* (9) 1969, 315–26, bibliography.

behaviour in the light of revelation and faith; the content of
the natural code of morals would not thereby be excluded
but rather, at least in its basic principles, implied; these
basic principles on the other hand may be regarded as also
contained in revelation.[4] The assumed parallel would imply
that dogmatic theology has teaching on faith as its object
(*de fide*) and moral theology teaching on morals (*de moribus*):
the teaching on faith treats of that which according to
revelation is true and must be accepted in faith, the teaching
on morals that which must be put into effect in the moral life
of the Christian. The teaching on faith refers to what must
be believed (*credenda*), the moral teaching to what must be
done (*agenda*). But may the Christian teaching be so split up?
If there is a teaching on Christian behaviour (*agere*), does it
not, at least in its basic tenets, belong also to the teaching on
faith (*de fide*)? For what constitutes Christian life and action
is in the last resort to be discovered from revelation and faith:
what is to be done (*agenda*) can also be part of what is to be
believed (*credenda*). In other words, to the content of faith
(*credenda*) can belong not only the truths about what has been
done (*facta*), but also about what is to be done (*agenda*). And
something similar can be said if we approach the question
from the other side. We don't indeed need the Trinity,
Christ or the eucharistic body of Christ in order to 'live';
yet it must not be forgotten that these 'truths' or 'facts' have
been revealed to us not so much for their own sakes as for
the sake of our relation to the realities expressed in them.
For this much is certainly true: our existence in the presence
of the Trinity, our calling in Christ and our sacramental
incorporation into him demand not only belief but also
action. *Fides* is concerned not only with events that have

[4]Note that the physical possibility of the natural knowledge of *God as origin
and goal* asserted by Vatican I implies also the possibility of the natural
knowledge of the basic principles of the natural moral law, according to the
express declaration of official spokesman, Gasser (Collectio Lac. 7, 133). But
according to the same Council God as origin and goal is the object not only
of possible natural knowledge, but also of revelation (cf. Denz.-Schönm.
3004 and 3005).

already taken place (*facta*), and *mores* refers not only to what should be done (*agenda*). A clean break between dogmatic and moral theology is theoretically and scientifically not possible.

Dogmatic theology as Christian anthropology: indicative and imperative

Dogmatic theology is *theology*, teaching about God and his historical self-revelation. Systematically and by the methods of human wisdom it tries to explore the reality and activity of God in accordance with his self-revelation through his word. Dogmatic theology asks: what is God and his love for man, what is the Three-in-Oneness of God and its relation to the meaning of man's life and the history of his salvation, what is the meaning of God becoming man and his work of redemption, what is the activity of God in faith, sacrament and Church, what is God's everlasting relation to us?

These questions show that dogmatic theology can and must be regarded as Christian anthropology also. God's revelation in the word is also the revelation of salvation,[5] that is, the revelation of God in so far as he works our salvation, and consequently the revelation of our salvation that God works. The object of attention, then, is man and his salvation, a salvation that God alone effects and that is yet at the same time the personal life of man himself. God is concerned in his revelation not so much with a self-revelation as such directed at an increase of theoretical knowledge on our part, but much more with the realization of our salvation that consists in the closest possible relationship between him and us. The divine reality that is proclaimed in the saving revelation is a vital factor (*existenzial*) of man's existence: he lives in the presence of the Trinity, with Christ the God-man and Redeemer, surrounded and sustained by his saving activity, intended for the perfection of the *Eschaton* which is already present. Man is all this; and dogmatic theology is to that extent theological anthropology.

[5]Cf. K. Rahner, 'Theologie und Anthropologie', in *Schriften zur Theologie*, VIII, 43–65, esp. 51.

But since the Christian-human reality is concerned with creatures, it is not only gift and grace; it is also a demand that man should accept it in its fullness and realize it in freedom. Theological anthropology is of necessity one single teaching about the 'is' and the 'ought' of the Christian, one single theology or dogmatic theology. And if the attempt is made to separate dogmatic theology and morals, the separation can never be a clean break, as if dogmatic theology existed exclusively for the Christian 'is' and moral theology for the Christian 'ought'. For the dogmatic teaching must become the morality of the Christian[6] and moral theology is theological anthropology translated from the indicative into the imperative.[7] But the imperative is just as much theological anthropology as the indicative, and belongs to the *one* theology of the Christian reality. The indicative and the imperative are related in such a fashion that they mutually imply each other and can only be fully understood as so implying each another.

Moral theology as 'developed' dogmatic theology

It is not only when we look at moral theology from the point of view of dogmatic theology, but also when we look at dogmatic theology from the point of view of moral theology that we see their inner connectedness and unity. Even the phenomenon of morality as such cannot be properly accounted for without a dogmatic theology. Morality is a basic phenomenon, a primary experience of every individual. Without this experience no one can understand moral concepts *as moral* whether they be natural or revealed. It is the experience of an inner tendency and direction towards an absolute which expresses itself as the *dictamen conscientiae*. But this explanation on its own is not sufficient for moral theology. For confrontation with an absolute, in conscience, is a confrontation with God, the triune God, when the

[6]See K. Rahner, *Lex. f. Theol. und Kirche*, III², 452.
[7]B. Schüller, *Gesetz und Freiheit*, Düsseldorf 1966, 46.

L

Father calls us through Christ in the holy Spirit to salvation. The mature human being always makes some answer to this call. He accepts or rejects the call to salvation in Christ. Consequently the experience of morality, of conscience, is ultimately a 'Christian' experience. It is simply the personal achievement of faith, or the extension of faith into moral action. We must, of course, remember that in the last resort the achievement of faith as well as the experience of morality cannot be fixed in concepts or schematized. (We will not here discuss the problem of how, on this theory, the achievement of faith and an experience of morality that goes beyond the natural order are possible without encountering the word of revelation, or how to treat the question, in what way acts, which are not in the actual and full sense, but only analogously, moral acts—i.e. 'light' acts—are 'Christian', be they acts of an adult, or of a child.) True morality is then a consequence and extension of the achievement of faith; and, like it, can be properly understood only from the theological and dogmatic point of view. Even the attempt to give the basic moral decision concrete form in the varying particular situations of one's life takes place through the dynamism generated by the personal achievement of faith. The effort to find moral norms for categorical action is the attempt of the believer, acting on his Christian faith and conscience, to discover courses of human action which constitute the imperatives corresponding to the indicatives of Christian anthropology.

From the theological point of view, therefore, it would not be quite correct to speak of an ethic which is 'presupposed' in the sense of an already existing 'natural' or philosophical ethic which would *later* be completed and re-shaped by theology and so in some way adequately accounted for. When theology attempts to clarify God's work of salvation which has been revealed, the attempt cannot succeed without philosophical effort, mainly because Christian salvation does not come about in a vacuum but in a created human being. God's revealed work of salvation cannot consequently be understood without philosophical reflection about this created human being. Therefore this philosophizing takes place *within* the frame of theology, which is attempting to come to an understanding of the salvation event in man.[7a] In this way the place of philosophical or 'natural' ethics is determined with reference to moral theology; it does not come before or continue alongside moral theology, but achieves its proper form within it. Moral theology as theological anthropology concerned with the morality of the Christian is impossible without philosophical reflection. Moral theology as a science is impossible without a 'natural' and philosophical understanding of what the moral law, moral obligation, personal act, etc., are.[8] But it must not be forgotten that ethical reflection takes place within moral theology as theology. This is the attempt to grasp the salvation revealed and offered to us which must be personally accepted and lived. Under this ethic is included not only the formal understanding of morality, but also the decision-making for concrete moral behaviour. 'Most moral rulings are not educed by the Church [or by theology— *author*] out of its purely Christian inheritance, but are rather the result of rational reflection about man and his life in society, or reaction to the good or bad experiences that follow on his behaviour. And these must be respected by the Christian as well as by the non-believer.'[9] The norms of the

---

[7a]See B. Welte, *Heilsverständnis—Philosophische Untersuchung einiger Voraussetzungen zum Verständnis des Christentums*, Freiburg 1966, 47: 'In a word, philosophy in itself is never theology. But its inclusion in sacred sciences is unavoidably theological. This is so, not because what is known is now absorbed by faith, but because revelation—accepted as revelation—demands that knowledge be subject to faith, and that one unite the two in the search for salvation.'

[8]Cf. B. Schüller, 'Zur theologischen Diskussion über die lex naturalis', *Theologie und Philosophie* (41) 1965, 481–503, esp. 492–500.

[9]A. Auer, 'Auf dem Wege zu einer Theologie der Arbeit', in *Theologie im Wandel*, Munich 1967, 564. Similarly J. Rief, *art. cit.*, 539; B. Schüller, *art. cit.* See also H. Conzelmann, *Grundriss der Theologie des Neuen Testamentes*, Munich 1967, 111: 'Moral teaching is given here, but it is not a new morality that is developed. Because there is no doubt about what morality is. The heathens know that as well as the Jews, according to *Romans* 2.'

natural moral code that philosophy indicates are regarded
by moral theology as ways of moral extension of the achievement of faith corresponding to the reality of the created
human being. In fact revelation has told him that he is
destined for salvation in Christ and lives in the reality of this
salvation.

Moral theology therefore proves to be, even in its philosophical reflection, theology of basically the same sort as
dogmatic theology. If one wishes to make a distinction
between the two, one must not only establish that dogmatic
theology is important for moral theology, but also the
reverse: moral theology is of service to dogmatic theology in
that it continues the work that dogmatic theology has begun
by assimilating and incorporating it in personal life, to give
concrete expression to the meaning of salvation (see below
III, 2).

The 'dogmatic' character and method of moral theology

In keeping with what has been said so far, the character
and method of moral theology are essentially the same as
those of dogmatic theology. This can be illustrated by two
typical cases.

In the first place, the basic propositions of moral theology
are, like those of dogmatic theology, at one and the same
time valid both as anthropological propositions and in the
context of the salvation event. Moral theology can, on the
basis of revelation and of the conclusions reached by its own
proper method, make statements that are anthropologically
valid: statements about the essence of morality, moral
perfection, moral law, the formal and material norms of the
moral life. But in all these statements, and in speaking about
the created human being with his moral law, his moral
imperatives, his relations with God, his fellow-man and
human society, moral theology is aware that such propositions have their full significance only in a context of salvation

history: otherwise they remain in a void. Moral theology will not indeed say after every statement that it is basically Christological and therefore to be understood in a context of salvation history, but that must somewhere be made quite clear, and moral theology must remain constantly aware of it. And not only that; moral theology will also make it quite clear that certain statements about man can be understood only in the context of salvation history. For instance, the idea of a moral law for man as a sinner and as a recipient of grace can only be made comprehensible in the perspective of salvation history. Similarly the full meaning of chastity and unchastity can only be presented in the perspective of salvation history; see for example the statements of Paul about the unchastity of Christians. (1 *Cor.* 6, 12–20.)

Secondly, moral theology is, like dogmatic theology, in its methodology both positive and speculative. As a positive science it examines the Scriptures, with the help of exegesis, to discover from them what, from the moral point of view, are the basic themes of Christian anthropology and also to find particular statements of this anthropology. Similarly it turns to the tradition of faith and doctrine and the magisterium of the Church to find what insights it can, by close reflection on the theological content and range of application of the statements found there. As a speculative science, moral theology, like dogmatic, does not create for itself a separate philosophical antechamber or annex, but attempts through speculation to penetrate more deeply into the truths which have been revealed. And there it has above all the task of discovering from the indicatives what are the imperatives that are virtually contained in them. Moreover, moral theology cannot be held to be going outside its proper field when it attempts to put into practice its awareness of Christian anthropology, even when this attempt takes it into the realm of the natural law of morals, where it must take cognizance of the 'profane' disciplines, like psychology, sociology, etc.

II. MORAL DOGMATIC THEOLOGY OR DOGMATIC MORAL THEOLOGY?

The preceding section on 'Moral theology as dogmatic theology' has demonstrated the theoretical and scientific unity of moral and dogmatic theology. But since a distinction in fact has been made and is convenient, there arises for moral theology the question of the importance of dogmatic theology for moral theology taken as a special discipline. This we will deal with in the next section (III below). There is, however, a further consideration. The treatment of any given theme in moral theology can be regarded as both moral theology (dogmatic moral theology) and as dogmatic theology (moral dogmatic theology). When such an exchange does not appear possible the reason may be that moral theology has not treated its particular theme exhaustively enough, perhaps because it is accustomed to leave this treatment to dogmatic theology. Under the heading of 'Moral dogmatic theology or dogmatic moral theology?' I would like to make some remarks about (1) the dogmatic theology of transcendental morality, and (2) the dogmatic theology of categorical morality.

On the dogmatic theology of transcendental morality

Moral theology that consciously and deliberately detaches itself from dogmatic theology is in danger of losing sight of the real and decisive element in Christian morality. History has shown that where morality has become excessively autonomous it concentrates one-sidedly on the moral act as a single action. And in so doing it tends all too easily to concern itself more or less exclusively with the categorical character of the moral act. It will pay less attention to the fact that it is the *perfection of the person* through the perfection of the act, and this achievement is a *supernatural and Christian* one. In these two elements is found the real depth of Christian morality which in the last resort can be understood only when it is seen to be 'dogmatic moral theology'. It is not, of course, concerned with the categorical diversity and separation of different virtues and their acts, that is, morality in the sense of correct categorical behaviour. For the self-completion of the person, which is, indeed, achieved through categorical actions, is, because of its supernatural and Christian relation with God, a transcendental reality, that is, it transcends all the categories of moral behaviour. Now it has always been realized, and in moral theology too, that behind the category question, what is just and what is unjust, what is chaste and what is unchaste, there lies a deeper problem, and that is whether in the different kinds of action the man himself is good or evil, whether he turns himself towards God or turns away from him, whether he lives or refuses to live the life of faith and love. The connected question has also been asked, that is, how the categorical moral acts in the different categories can be supernatural or meritorious in the strict sense. It must also be said that these have been regarded as primarily dogmatic problems and for that reason given less attention in moral theology. Moreover, the concept of 'the transcendental' in the perfection of the Christian life has been more strongly emphasized in theology only in recent times, and here again primarily in dogmatic theology.

The absoluteness of individual moral demands is an indication of the contingence of man in the face of God. The performance of an individual moral action affects the quality of the whole person to the extent that he as agent realizes himself as a person and accepts his contingence. Through the individual moral act the human being progresses from invitation through free decision to commitment in freedom. The self-realization in freedom is achieved through the free choice of a categorical act which is to be done. We might add that the individual realizes a personal freedom, that is, freedom of choice, in carrying out a categorical action as such, but achieves basic freedom in the self-completion which is contained in the performance of this act. For the understanding of this state of affairs it is helpful to remember that, in place of the earlier distinctions between actual, virtual and habitual intention, differences between the various forms and layers of consciousness (and conscience) have been worked out with more and more refinement by philosophical and theological anthropology. It has become clear that the performance of a categorical action as such is accessible to consciousness operating through categories and schemata. There we are concerned with freedom of choice. On the other hand, the self-completion which is achieved through such an act, and which belongs to the realm of transcendental basic freedom is a matter for the transcendental consciousness, which is not confined by schemata, and it thereby remains closed and inaccessible to any sort of adequate, schematic examination.

Because the absolute claim of God on man is always made effective as the call through grace to salvation in communion with the Trinity, it is clear that the decisive element in morality is the willing acceptance of responsibility by the self as one who has been called by the God of our salvation. The categorical moral acts are the expression of acceptance of God's call to salvation. This acceptance emerges as the willing self-disposal of the whole person in transcendental basic freedom, in the realm of the consciousness that is not confined to categories. Though the acceptance itself is something that goes beyond the categories, it does nevertheless take place through some categorical moral act. And since all true morality implies absolute adhesion and commitment, there is no genuine morality in categorical acts of everyday life without the free acceptance of God's call to salvation, the ready disposal of the self to the call of God.

True morality, then, the commitment to the Absolute Being in the fulfilment of a concrete demand, always contains within itself a 'theologal life' and is that life's practical expression. The immediacy of the relationship to God in hoping and loving faith is what gives the moral life its real depth, because it is this relationship, with its transcendental consciousness and freedom that inspires and sustains the moral achievement. We must not think of the moral life in all its different categories as existing *alongside* the 'theologal' life of relationship to God in faith, hope and charity; they exist *in* one another. (When we talk of *explicit* acts of faith, hope and charity, we are really speaking about categorical religious acts, which as such are at the same time moral acts, in which the self-achievement of theologal life, which is non-reflex and on which no adequate reflection is possible, seeks to express itself.) The coincidence of human morality and 'theologal' life becomes indeed full *identity* in the case of Christian love of the neighbour. In this case the love of the neighbour, as the supernatural love of God, inspires and sustains all right behaviour to the neighbour, and not only the works of kindness and mercy, but also those of justice.

Here we must introduce another concept in 'dogmatic moral theology', that of the following of Christ. In the numerous biblical studies in recent years on this concept[10] attention has been drawn to the fact that the disciples after the Resurrection and the later Christians distinguished the following of Christ from association with the Lord in the fulfilment of his mission on earth and sharing in his life up to the carrying of the cross. The following of Christ means simply to be a Christian. But that in turn means to enrol oneself for the Lord in faith and love, to be one and to remain one with him, to take on his spirit which will urge us on in the denial, mortification and crucifixion of the sinful ego. The following of Christ is basically not this or that categorical act of Christain behaviour, but the transcendental commitment of the self. All true morality then, is the

[10]See E. Neuhäusler, *Anspruch und Antwort Gottes,* Düsseldorf 1962, 186–214; E. Larsson, *Christus als Vorbild,* Uppsala 1962; A. Schulz, *Nachfolgen und Nachahmen,* Munich 1962; H. Zimmermann, 'Christus nachfolgen', *Theologie und Glaube* (53) 1963, 241–68; T. Aerts, 'Suivre Jésus', *Eph. Théol. Lov.* (42) 1966, 476–512; R. Thysman, 'L'Éthique de l'Imitation du Christ dans le N.T.', *Eph. Théol. Lov.* (42) 1966, 138–75; H. D. Betz, *Nachfolge und Nachahmung im Neuen Testament,* Tübingen 1967; M. Hengel, *Nachfolge und Charisma,* Berlin 1968.

following of Christ, because it is sustained by this transcendental commitment; not this or that way of behaviour
which could be taken to be an imitation of Christ's way of
behaviour in certain circumstances, but that true moral
behaviour which is in harmony with the spirit of Christ and
thereby 'imitates' the attitude of Christ. The commitment
to the following of Christ, that is, the commitment of hoping
and loving faith, is in fact that primal force which we *more
abstractly* describe as basic conscience (*Synteresis*). It is by
this force we are carried along when we try to do the
categorically good act in a particular situation in life; we bow
before it, in basic freedom and transcendental consciousness,
when we actually do good in the concrete situation.

Faith and the following of Christ make a man face up to
the situation of the *Eschaton*, the end of time. One often
hears it said that it is this confrontation which explains the
radical nature of Christian morality, as expressed for example
in the Sermon on the Mount. That is not wrong; but what
do *Eschaton* and 'radical nature' mean? It may well be that
here and there in the New Testament writings an expectation
of the fast approaching end explains a certain radical
tendency, perhaps in 1 Corinthians 7 for example. But
however that may be, we understand the *Eschaton* as the
kingship of God in us already begun with the coming of
Christ, the domination of God growing stronger and stronger
until the final consummation. This situation, radically
different from that of the self-centred man who has through
the Fall turned away from his home in God, demands that
man be absolutely genuine and that his morality be, in this
sense, radical. This then is the transcendental eschatological
commitment that determines, inspires and sustains the
categorical morality in everyday life. And this eschatological
attitude and significance is alive in all true Christian
morality.

What has been said so far about 'transcendental' morality
obviously needs a certain modification. Apart altogether
from the question whether there is such a thing as human

behaviour and action that goes on completely outside the sphere of morality (it seems more probable that in the case of conscious action we are also always conscious of the moral aspect of our action, even if there isn't much reflection), we have to remember the fact that not all moral action is to the same degree personal, that is, proceeds from the centre of the personality. In many cases our moral activity goes on at the surface, as it were, of the personality; it is still personal and is still connected with the centre of the personality, but the connection is *only* 'superficial'. Since 'transcendental' Christian morality in its proper nature is realized in the centre of personality of the human being, it affects 'superficial' moral behaviour only in 'superficial' fashion; that is, the Christian commitment enters into moral behaviour to animate and sustain it with less force and decisiveness.

On the dogmatic theology of categorical morality

The question of categorical morality is, like that of transcendental morality, one of those basic themes of moral theology which, when they are really theologically handled reveal an unmistakably 'dogmatic' character. It is precisely the transcendental 'Christianness' of Christian morality that gives meaning to discussion of the radical nature of that morality at the categorical level. This implies two things: firstly, that categorical Christian behaviour must give proof of the basic selfless decision for God and the neighbour in the holy Spirit; and then, secondly, that for this very reason the created reality which comes into being through the concrete act should not be treated offhandedly nor regarded as indifferent but according to its degree of significance should be taken seriously in a world which is in the last analysis personal or interpersonal. The 'Christianness' of categorical Christian morality would not then consist in a particular 'Christian moral code', as the Sermon on the Mount has often been presented. In that respect, one might say, the efforts of the last few decades to return at last to a 'Christian' morality have been on occasion somewhat one-sided. But now, under the influence of secularizing tendencies, moral theology has begun to free itself again from a certain one-sidedness in its 'Christianizing'; and it must take care that it does not again lose sight of its true Christian nature. That the categorical dimensions of moral behaviour are substantially equivalent to those of proper human behaviour pure and simple and do not derive from a special 'Christian moral code'[11] is in keeping not only with sound theological tradition but also with the Scriptures. A reading of Paul, for instance, reveals no insistence on a special 'Christian' rather than a 'human' moral code. This, however, does not mean that the apostle does not proceed critically as he takes over existing Jewish or pagan catalogues of virtues or vices. As a Christian he excises what is not Christian, because it is not truly 'human' (polytheism in the worship of house-gods, for instance), and at the same time he demands that a 'Christian', because 'human', form should be given to existing social institutions and conventions (for example, the demand for love between husband and wife, in spite of the subordination of the woman, and between master and slave). The distinction which Paul wants to emphasize in morality is not that between a 'Christian' and a 'human' moral code, but that between the 'new' man of the spirit (*pneuma*), who lives according to the moral code of true humanity, and the man of the flesh (*sarx*), who in his sinful self-centredness will not accept the demands of morality.

Moral theology must, then, in its discovery of the categorical norms, proceed largely by means of the ordinary disciplines of human thought, in spite of its theological ('dogmatic') character. The attempt that has sometimes been made to derive sexual or marital morality from the mystery of the Trinity or the Church in her relation to Christ produces no conviction. Human thought cannot, however, be reduced to the purely *a priori*. Nowadays the only moral norms which are regarded as *a priori* in the fullest sense are those most

[11]See note 9 above

general ones which are demonstrated by the transcendental method and which one implicitly affirms even when one disputes them.[12] The majority of moral norms on the other hand presume some experience of the particular area of application, with all its relevant factors, cultural and otherwise. There will be a certain amount of variety and diversification in such experience, with a corresponding variation in the discovery of norms. Besides, even though one must emphasize that there is a *correspondence* between the moral norm and the concrete reality, this does not imply that it is possible to *deduce logically* ethical norms from the concrete reality. (One cannot derive 'ought' categories from 'is' categories, one can only 'intuit' them, grasp them.) No theological method is capable of simply getting rid of the difficulties encountered in the attempt to find categorical norms.

Moral theology must indeed, because it is ('dogmatic') theology, attempt to go back to the Scriptures for light on the problems of categorical morality. But there is need of thorough, careful exegesis not only in the examination of the Old Testament but also in that of the New. It can be shown that Christ, just like Paul and John, made a radical demand for selfless love in every sphere of life, and one can find the corresponding 'ethical models' to serve as concrete directives for certain concrete circumstances.[13] Such concrete directives are sometimes not only expressed in the form of hyperbole, as for example in the Sermon on the Mount, and for that reason to be examined for their true value as statements, but they are also on occasion undoubtedly demands which are conditioned by their age, as for example Paul's demands for the subordination of women in the Church assembly and in marriage. And so exegesis demands that we determine carefully which concrete moral directives of the New Testament

[12]Cf. L. M. Weber, 'Ethische Probleme der Biotechnik und Anthropotechnik', *Arzt und Christ* (11) 1965, 231.

[13]Cf. J. Blank, 'New Testament Morality and Modern Moral Theology' *Concilium* (3) 1967, 6–12.

are conditioned by their age, or are perhaps only hypothetical and not definitive statements.

Similarly the *Church*, whether it be the whole assembly of the People of God or the official Church, has no other access to the questions of categorical morality than that of human understanding, so long as these questions are not dealt with by revelation too. She is not released from the difficulties indicated in the 'human' discovery of moral norms. The Church has not been promised controlling inspiration by the holy Spirit as guide and guarantee in her teaching and proclamation of categorical morality, but rather the support of this Spirit who will prevent the Church from *finally and definitively* falling into error. This support implies that even where definitiveness is not suggested, the presumption for the correctness of the teaching stands until the opposite should become clear. This consideration is also important where the Church goes back to her own tradition and teaching in the search for the proper categorical norm. But in establishing the range of application of such a tradition or teaching one must also note to what extent it is conditioned by its age and intended for a definite social situation and its historically conditioned understanding.

The Christian effort in regard to correct categorical morality is then very similar to the ordinary human effort. It is, however, theologically important that this human effort should be basically *Christian*. It is informed by the transcendental dynamism of Christian faith and love. It is the effort of a man who through his categorical faith is aware of his situation of tension between *sarx* and *pneuma*. The Christian will, because of his knowledge of Christ and his presence, sense the realities of salvation which are implicit in daily life and action. And when he looks at the person of Christ he realizes with regard to the concrete reality what the commitment of selfless, loving faith means in the concrete. And so the 'human' categorical morality, which the Christian seeks and finds, whether it be a 'general' norm of moral behaviour or actual behaviour in a given situation, is basically Christian and at its deepest level something which is sought out and discovered to be for this person the incarnation and expression of his Christianity. It is never just 'human', but always 'Christian' as well. That does not take away from the fact that it is the 'human' moral concepts which in the first place allow us to understand the statements of revelation on moral values and moral life.

Even where moral knowledge is not attained by the discursive method or exact logical argument but through a sort of perception or intuition, it still comes into being through the transcendental dynamism of Christian faith and love, and in the light of the categorical Christian consciousness of faith. Consequently Karl Rahner is right to call the moral instinct which is active in perception or intuition, a 'moral instinct of faith', which without full analytical reflection illuminates what is 'objectively' right in a proper decision.[14] For a similar idea E. Schillebeeckx points to the statement of Vatican II (*Gaudium et spes*, 46), that the problems of our time must be solved 'in the light of the Gospel and human experience'.[15] He puts the accent first on the necessity of 'human experience'; for ethical imperatives that are commensurate with the situation 'take their rise from very practical experience in life and they impose themselves because they are based on the clear evidence of experience. Only then are they thought through systematically, and critically examined, and clothed in the language of theology and the magisterium'. This statement emphasizes the true 'humanity' of the empirically based imperatives. And yet these imperatives are 'Christian'. Schillebeeckx observes how it is precisely the 'Christianness' of the Christian which makes him feel the contrast between a given social situation and the situation as it should be, even when it is not yet clear what practical steps should be taken.

But categorical faith has a further significance for cate-

[14]K. Rahner, 'Zum Problem der genetischen Manipulation' in *Schriften zur Theologie*, VIII, 303 f.

[15]See E. Schillebeeckx, 'The Magisterium and the World of Politics', *Concilium* (4) 1968, 12–21.

gorical Christian morality. For the *realities of the faith* must be actualized by each Christian for himself. The person of Christ, the holy Ghost at work in us, the Christian community, the hierarchical Church, the sacraments, Christian anthropology—all these cannot remain without effect on the categorical morality of the Christian as long as his morality corresponds to the reality of his faith. Christian motives, as for example for chastity (cf. 1 *Cor.* 6:12–20) and for truthfulness (*Eph.* 4:25), give categorical morality a special significance and help in its performance. But the realities of faith also have an influence on the content of categorical morality, without of course calling in question the fundamental 'humanity' of Christian morality or establishing a morality that contradicts this humanity. The knowledge of the person and work of Christ, life in a Christian community, hearkening to the holy Spirit etc., will all combine to make the 'human' ethic more determinate. Living in Christ will, for instance, help towards a fuller understanding of the meaning of the cross in the life of selfless love and of unconditional openness to the call of God and the demands of the concrete situation. Such an understanding cannot but have practical consequences.

Among the realities of faith one in particular must be singled out, and that is the work of the holy Spirit in us (cf. *Rom.* 5:5 and *Rom.* 8), the 'gratia Spiritus Sancti', which St Thomas calls the primary element in the New Law.[16] Grace in this sense is obviously not something static, something poured in, but the existential factor, the instrument of the Spirit who is at work in us in many different ways. This Spirit 'moves' each of us, in the Christian community and as a member of it, in accordance with our own character and situation and in accordance with our personal vocation, and for that very reason forces us to go beyond what can be described as the general requirements of Christian morality for everyone. Tradition has recognized a guidance of the holy

---

[16]*S. theol.* I-II, q. 106, art. 1s.

Spirit, the theology of which Karl Rahner has attempted to expound as 'formal existential ethic'.[17] According to this interpretation one is justified in seeing grace as the highest and final 'form' of man, which itself presupposes the humanity of the individual on whom grace has been conferred. But if this is the case, the grace of the holy Spirit who is at work in us must be described as the real norm of Christian behaviour, categorical behaviour included. It includes the 'human' morality of Christian behaviour. And because of this grace the individual, in his limited fashion and in accordance with his personal character and vocation, can be the image of the God-man Jesus Christ who is the model and norm of all Christian behaviour.

III. TWO INCOMPLETE AND COMPLEMENTARY DISCIPLINES.

The remarks made on the dogmatic theology of transcendental and categorical morality should have provided the justification for the question 'moral dogmatic theology or dogmatic moral theology' and so again have shown the theoretical unity of the two disciplines. If we regard moral theology as also dogmatic theology, yet for practical reasons maintain the separation of the two, the two disciplines are obviously to be understood as partial and complementary. As such they necessarily have a certain relation to one another and importance for one another. This we would like to investigate in what follows, although it is the importance of dogmatic theology for moral theology that interests us primarily. We must then consider the following: 1. the importance of dogmatic theology for moral theology, 2. The importance of moral for dogmatic theology, 3. Common problems.

[17]K. Rahner, 'On the Question of a Formal Existential Ethics', *Theological Investigations,* II (tr. K. H. Krüger), London 1963, 217– 35; *id., Das Dynamische in der Kirche,* Freiburg/Br. 1960[2], 100–136.

M

The importance of dogmatic theology for moral theology

If the self-revelation of God in the Christian tradition has a purpose beyond itself, being the work of our salvation, dogmatic theology must choose its themes in accordance with this truth, and when the choice is made, must place the emphasis accordingly too. Dogmatic theology can for instance deal equally well with the question of what happened to Christ, body and soul, at the moment of death, or with the question of how one is to understand the unity of God and man in Christ. But there is no doubt that the second question is more important for the understanding of the mystery of salvation than the first. A dogmatic theology that takes account of the purpose of the divine self-revelation, and in the light of it chooses its themes, will thus be directed in its selection of subject and the emphasis it gives. Dogmatic theology can also deal with this question of what happened to Christ, body and soul, at the moment of death, and with the question of the significance of this death in God's plan of salvation and in the mystery of Christ. Yet the dogmatic theologian who prefers to concentrate on the first rather than the second question will meet with little understanding from his hearers or readers, unless perhaps he wants to prove himself to be a specialist in the most recherché problems. Theologians have not perhaps always paid sufficient attention to God's intention in his self-revelation and its significance for theology when choosing their themes and placing their emphasis. But the more dogmatic theology does take account of God's plan in revelation for its choice of theme and emphasis, the closer it comes to the line of thought that moral theology can continue in its own way, and the more important it becomes for moral theology.

Consequently a dogmatic theology that consciously sees itself as teaching about God's work of salvation and call to us in Christ, and regards this as a central theme, prepares the way for a truly Christian moral theology. Moral theology will then all the more easily treat as its central question that of

perceiving and answering the call and the personal acceptance of the divine work of salvation in everyday Christian
life. The answer to the question, what does the separation of
body and soul in the death of Christ really mean, will not
prove very fruitful for moral theology. On the other hand,
the answer to the question of the real significance of the death
and resurrection of Christ, what meaning for salvation and
what saving power they have, provides material for the most
fruitful reflection in moral theology. Quite a few moral
theologians have tried to see the sacramental reality of the
Church and especially the seven sacraments as the basis of
Christian morality and the Christian ethos. Dogmatic teaching on how the sacraments work was not ignored in this
attempt, and yet a much stronger concentration on the
specific significance (and ultimately the significance for salvation) of the individual sacraments would have been more
important and helpful. In the measure that dogmatic
theology does this work can moral theology—if it does not
take on the work itself—work out and present the sacramental ethos of the Christian life.

Since, then, dogmatic theology is essentially theological
anthropology (see above I, 2), it will not spend so much time
in speculating about the nature of the God who is revealed to
us and of the 'facts' of the salvation-event, but will rather
turn its attention to the significance of this God and of his
acts for our salvation, because this is a vital factor in man's
existence. Theology will try to show how God's loving act of
salvation does its work within man's nature. And so it helps
moral theology to come nearer to a solution of the fundamental question about the 'human naturalness' and the 'Christianness' of Christian morality. Dogmatic theology will
attempt to fathom the mystery of how the saving act of God
(the grace of the holy Spirit, faith and love) and man's free
self-realization can work together in undivided unity and yet
remain unconfused; in so doing theology will make use of an
anthropology which is concerned with human achievement,
which is psychological and especially philosophical, and is

itself illuminated by theology. Moral theology would come thereby to a deeper understanding and a more realistic evaluation of the moral behaviour of the Christian, and to a more fundamental grasp of the nature and significance of Christian transcendental and categorical morality (see above II).

Dogmatic theology, which recognizes the decisive importance of revelation for the salvation of man in Christ, is at the present time, in the form of 'political' theology, turning its attention more and more to the significance in salvation history of the Christian's 'secular' interest in the world.[18] Such a theology not only enables moral theology to see the relation of the Christian to the world in a new light. It also allows moral theology to give a more competent judgement on certain attitudes of the Christian to the world, above all on his 'engagement' for the world and his active participation in it, as he attempts to help in its progress and development.

One could perhaps summarize the position as follows: dogmatic theology turns its attention both to questions that are of fundamental importance for a moral theology of the Christian life, and also to questions within this Christian life itself, like the acceptance of grace, faith, love; and moral theology then endeavours to make these more concrete. Dogmatic theology, in order to be able to answer the questions that are put to it satisfactorily, turns not only to the data of revelation but also to the results of human research and reflection, as for example those of philosophical and psychological anthropology. A dogmatic theology which works in this fashion does not put itself expressly at the service of moral theology; but it is of the greatest importance for moral theology in that moral theology builds on the results of dogmatic theology in its reflections on the phenomenon of Christian morality.

[18]Cf. J. B. Metz, *Zur Theologie der Welt*, Mainz/Munich., 1968: *id.*, 'The Church's Social Function in the Light of "Political Theology" ', *Concilium* (4) 1968, 3–11.

The importance of moral theology for dogmatic theology

The importance of moral for dogmatic theology corresponds essentially to the importance of dogmatic for moral theology. This importance is chiefly that it *carries further* the work of dogmatic theology which is incomplete and remains at a higher level of speculation and abstraction. Besides that it takes up again the themes of dogmatic theology, not simply as presuppositions or for the sake of repetition, but to study them with a view to the practical work of salvation in everyday life. It then takes this study as its point of departure for its reflection on the phenomenon of Christian morality. This reflection presupposes the experience of Christian morality. Moral theology can carry out this task only because it, more than dogmatic theology, draws on the results of various 'profane' disciplines and on experience.

So, for example, dogmatic theology will treat of God's will of universal salvation, of God's saving call to the individual, of faith and love as at once divine gift and human achievement, of the total dedication of the individual in every moment and in every action to the God who calls him. Moral theology will be more concerned with explaining what God's saving call implies for the Christian conscience in itself (*synteresis*), for this conscience in particular situations (*syneidesis*) and for the Christian discovery of moral norms (*scientia moralis*). For what is described in philosophical ethics as the conscience in itself is in the true Christian the expression of his profound and total commitment to the following of Christ in faith and love (see above II, 1). The categorical knowledge of conscience in the particular situation takes place not only through the dynamism and in the light of the basic Christian conscience, but is besides a free personal reaction to the grace-giving action of the Spirit within, and to the visible presentation of a norm of Christian action in the Christian community and in the official Church. And the discovery of 'general' moral norms, however much it is a matter for the ordinary processes of human thought, must also be seen as a disposition to look for God's call to salvation in the concrete circumstances of daily life (see above I, 3 and II, 2); and this, of course, is impossible without reference to the essentially Christian realities.

Dogmatic theology will, again, speak of the necessity of the actual presence of the saving power of Christ in everyday Christian life. Moral theology has then to work out, on the basis of the analysis of the phenomenon of morality, of anthropological reflection on personal fulfilment and of the results of psychological research, in what act of the Christian the saving power of Christ is made evident and to what degree (see above II, 1). It will attempt to describe the relation of this saving presence to the substance of the act, the psychological situation of the agent and the degree of personal self-fulfilment in question. It should be clear that in this way moral theology treats the pressing questions of sin and good works in the Christian life as the continuation of basic themes of dogmatic theology.

Again, dogmatic theology will show how necessary it is that the Christian acceptance of salvation finds its incarnation and expression in the proper realization of the potentialities of man in the world. Moral theology must reduce this to practice. What is the 'proper' realization in this case? Moral theology cannot answer this question without reflecting on scriptural utterances on morality and on the range of application of these utterances; but it must also take into account what it means to be human, the way in which various human cultures are conditioned, the experience of different ways of behaviour, the insights of psychology and sociology etc. Here the work of moral theology in carrying dogmatic theology further and making it more concrete becomes more than obvious. But this activity will soon reach its own limits in a number of questions, especially in this technical age of ours. The technical knowledge on which moral rule-giving must be based, the ability to recognize and evaluate the implications and consequences of certain courses of action, will simply not be within the grasp of the represen-

tatives of moral theology. The Christians who have the
necessary technical knowledge will in that case best work out
for themselves the human action which will be the incarnation of the Christian reality of salvation. The science of
moral theology (and the teaching Church) will in many
cases be able to present only more or less formal principles
and guiding lines together with a few model cases of proper
behaviour. The final reduction of the dogmatic statement at
any rate takes place in *every* case through a judgement of conscience which is responsibly taken and which makes use of the
relevant aids to a proper formation of conscience, and this
judgement illuminates and accompanies all Christian action.

Common problems

We have found the chief importance of moral theology for
dogmatic theology in its continuation and concrete application of dogmatic theology, its more direct confrontation
with the realities of practical life. But moral theology has a
further significance for dogmatic theology, for when once the
separation has been made, moral theology's approach to the
salvation event, which is of its nature more concrete and
closer to real life, can on occasion have its effect on dogmatic
theology. Moral theology's attitude to sin, for instance, is
more concrete and practical. Consequently it can on occasion
cause dogmatic theology, with its tendency to remain on a
higher level of abstraction, to evolve new formulae in order
to avoid serious misunderstandings.

This consideration of a possible effect of moral theology on
dogmatic theology leads to a further assertion. There are
questions which of their nature can only be solved by both
disciplines working together. This is not to ask that both sit
down to the same table together but rather that both disciplines make their own contributions to the one theme
thereby providing a solution to the question which interests
them both. An example is the importance of statements of
the Church's magisterium on questions of the natural moral
law. In so far as an ecclesiological question is here involved,

dogmatic theology is clearly competent. But anyone who
considers how complex the problem of the natural moral law
is in itself, how many elements of human reality must be
kept in mind in laying down the norms of the natural law,
how difficult it is to reach a decision on the range of application of statements of the natural law, will realize that too
much is being asked of the dogmatic theologian. Even recourse to the statements of Scripture or the Church magisterium on questions of the natural law cannot relieve him of
the necessity for an introduction by moral theology into the
complex question of the natural moral law. Ecclesiology and
moral theology together must work out the conditions for a
fair and satisfactory solution of the question 'Magisterium
and natural law'.

It can scarcely be doubted that in the course of the last few
decades moral theology has re-discovered its theological
character. A question to which less attention has been paid
in this re-discovery is to what extent this theological character can be described as dogmatic.[19] There is no doubt that
this re-discovery was an important one; moral and dogmatic
theology had been separated on purely practical grounds.
There should also be no doubt that this re-discovery was a
necessary one—because without it the 'Christianness' of
Christian morality could remain concealed, its foundations in
God's revelation and work of salvation could be overlooked,
and its true significance be forgotten with its salvific power
for the daily life of the Christian in the proclamation of
Christian morality.

Or is it sufficient that dogmatic theology should look after
the 'theological', 'dogmatic' aspects of the problems of moral
theology? Against this solution there is first the fact that dogmatic theology, because it is a discipline which is in fact
separate from moral theology will, in general, concern itself
less with the problems of moral theology and for that reason

---

[19]K. Rahner deals with this very question in the *Lexikon* article already
referred to.

will not in fact convey or try to express the dogmatic aspect of moral theology. Secondly there is the fact that a moral theology which does not itself try to make its dogmatic character evident ultimately does not look like theology and in the end, because of that, does not look Christian.

Consequently, when moral and dogmatic theology are treated as separate though complementary disciplines, they must both work in the awareness of their mutual importance. The aims and efforts of dogmatic theology will always be directed towards the realization of the mystery of salvation in the Christian life; that is, it will lead on to moral theology. Moral theology will also be concerned with the realization of the mystery of salvation in Christian life, and for that reason it must take the statements of dogmatic theology that touch on the Christian life as its starting point and from these try to make the moral life comprehensible. And since there is no clear boundary between dogmatic and moral theology, moral theology, in harmony with dogmatic theology, will very often determine pragmatically how far it will go in its detailed realization of its theological and dogmatic character.

7　On the Theology of Human Progress[1]

When the moral theologian in a series of theological lectures speaks of human progress, he must confine himself to a theme in moral theology which he can presume has not already been appropriated by the dogmatic theologian. For it is a fact that in contemporary theology the dogmatic and moral theologian deal with themes like this one in more or less the same way. In order to avoid overlapping we shall deal with the theology of human progress under an aspect which traditionally belongs quite clearly to the field of moral theology.

The description in Section I of some traditional difficulties in the way of an adequate moral theological evaluation of human progress is followed by Section II in which progress is shown as a mandate and consequently a moral duty of man. Then in Section III come considerations of the 'moral standardization' of human progress, and in Section IV the relation is recognized between a valid appraisal of progress and a dynamic understanding of the moral philosophy. A comprehensive reflection on the religious-ethical character of human progress forms the conclusion in Section V.

I. DIFFICULTIES CONFRONTING A MORAL THEOLOGICAL EVALUATION OF HUMAN PROGRESS

The fact must not be overlooked that traditional moral theology has experienced difficulty in ascribing sufficient value to human progress in the sense of the active development and evolution of man and his world. It has regarded

[1]One of a series of lectures of an interdisciplinary course on the theology of human progress given at the Pontifical Gregorian University, Rome, January, 1969.

this active development primarily as of very relative and purely secular value in contrast to the absolute and non-secular value of the moral, the religious and the supernatural. One is conscious here of a tension that obstructed a moral evaluation of the development of man and universe—whose worth was always qualified as purely natural, purely secular, purely immanent; the word 'purely' is significant. Nevertheless the continuing development of the human world was understood as an objective manifestation of the greatness of the Creator and thus as the glorification of God. One was correspondingly aware of the possibility that man was capable of a subjective understanding of the development of creation as the glorification of the Creator. Yet the active development of man and his world appears simply as the setting in which man can exercise religious-ethical motives. Thus progress may bear an *indirect* relationship to morality and religiosity; but an interior and direct relationship to absolute values is not apparent.

In this view the supernatural above all appears as that value, in opposition to the merely secular, which man must realize as the absolute. The reality of grace may be understood as this 'supernatural' of sole importance—be it only very narrowly regarded as an 'it' or rather as the personal relationship between God calling to salvation and man accepting this call. Against this unique value of the supernatural the value of human progress in this world—as being only secular—is extraordinarily relative. Should one in the development of the world, and by means of it, make a supernatural gain, the earthly progress appears of indifferent value as against the supernatural.

One often speaks instead of the value of the supernatural, of the value of the moral, which is regarded as the absolute value in contrast to the relative human values. However, this absolute value of the moral is not perceived in the active development of man himself and of his world, but rather in the moral method followed in achieving progress. The progress itself is only of value in the realm of the secular—

of science, of technology, of biological-psychological life, of the material, etc. The progress itself does not bear an intimate and direct relationship to the moral value which man in his progress at any rate achieves. Progress does not appear as a moral task; but as being able to provide the material for a man who acts properly to achieve moral worth, to live a virtuous and supernaturally worthy life.

Another definition, which basically means the same thing, states that the sole absolute and lasting value is fulfilment of the will of God. Instead of 'will of God' we should perhaps say 'moral order'. This will of God, the moral order, is somehow regarded as a static gift and obligation. It is to be observed in the continuing development of the human world; but progress itself remains in an indifferent position, in so far as it is without intrinsic relationship to the will of God.

It will scarcely be denied that the tension between the 'absolute' values and the merely secular values has been widely regarded more or less in the way described here—if this is perhaps a somewhat one-sided description. And certainly in this view the active progress of man and his world belongs among the purely secular, purely immanent, purely relative values. Perhaps without undue exaggeration the position could be stated as follows: there were two mutually competitive relationships of man—his horizontal relationship to his fellow-men and to the world on one side and his vertical relationship to the absolute on the other. But both relationships were largely regarded as *categorical* relationships, which exist alongside each other and because of this can and must enter into competition with each other. From this it is also clear that the higher will win the day over the less high—that the latter, because it is in competition with the former, becomes relative and indifferent.

II. PROGRESS AS A MANDATE FOR MAN

The difficulties which in the past often stood in the way of an adequate moral evaluation of human progress, arose primarily because the horizontal and vertical relationships of man were regarded as categorical and thus as being in competition. However, the vertical relationship of man to the Absolute must be understood as a primarily transcendental one when considered in connection with the horizontal relationship man-world. As such it does not enter into competition with the categorical relationship of man to the age he lives in and to the world, but exists and is achieved precisely *in* the realization of the horizontal reality of mankind. If one can speak of a possible rivalry, it is not between the horizontal secularity of man and the vertical relationship with God of man as a totality, as a person, but between worship and meditation on the one hand and 'worldly' efficacy on the other. But worship and meditation do not form the real and transcendental relationship of man to God; they belong rather to his categorical and horizontal self-realization. Both, that is the categorical self-realization in worship and meditation as well as the categorical 'worldly' efficacy, are means of self-realization in which and through which the transcendental relationship to God can be achieved. The 'absolute' and 'supernatural' worth is not actually to be sought in the categorical acts of worship and meditation, but in that relationship to the Absolute, to God, to Christ, which lives and operates in categorical acts— worldly reality as well as worship and meditation.

In the categorical view what does the creation of this world require with regard to the world itself? Just this one thing; that man and his world—and this as the world of mankind—should *be*; we can put it like this—that man should be *human*, i.e. a person in this world. But this means that man as a person should develop the world—the world, that is, of men and, in their service, the rest of the world, developing himself thereby. But that implies progress, progressive humanization of the man-world reality, i.e. of mankind and his world. In the fulfilment of this mandate of creation and by means of it man realizes himself as a person in the vertical direction; he does this, finally, not in the categorical but in the transcendental sense.

This reflection obviously implies a precise concept of the so-called natural moral law according to which, it must be unequivocally recognized that man's duty lies in being man, in being himself. This natural law does not consist merely in a collection of demands or orders to be accepted—but rather in the demand to accept oneself as a mandate from the Creator. The concept of the natural moral law as produced as it were above and beyond the creation of mankind (and his world) to which it is in some way 'added', in the sense of a collection of principles or demands, would be basically voluntaristic and thus the direct opposite to natural law. Man is supposed to be a man, a man among men, a man of this world, a worldly man; such is—in a horizontal categorical respect—the content of the natural law. What this means in concrete terms it is up to man, i.e. humanity, to find out for himself; that belongs to the essence of the natural moral law as the law of the nature of man.[1a] Should this 'nature of man' be more closely defined, we must take into consideration that man is a *personal* and *historical* being.

The fact that man—as the image of God (*Gen.* 1)—is a *person* means not merely that he can accept, preserve, contemplate mankind, the world of men and himself as a given reality, but rather that he should grasp it, have control over it, shape it, develop it, increasingly and in a more active fashion stamp it with his own nature—in other words increasingly 'humanize' it. Man and his world are not simply actuality, but also potentiality; the given reality and possible development are a single actuality and are in the

---

[1a] This is also true of the Church's knowledge of the natural law—even of the official Church, which does not arrive at a knowledge of the natural law via some private revelation, but by human effort. Where particular truths of the natural law appear in revelation, a second source of knowledge of these truths is thereby provided. Naturally, the evaluation of this source demands exact exegesis. Here we will not tackle the difficult question of the theological value of the norms of the natural law, historically formulated in the Church—be it among the faithful, the theologians, or the Magisterium. Clearly, for a knowledge of the natural law as treated above, the norms of the natural law which have developed in the ecclesial community based on revelation and moral perception must be considered according to their theological value.

charge of man as created person-in-world. As person-in-world, man has to make an ever fresh attempt to discover in what way man's conduct, the formation of human society and the control and 'utilization' of the reality of the world in the service of mankind can be truly human, can measure up to the dignity of man as a person in this reality. In other words; what kind of progress can be called 'human' progress in the true sense of the word? In so far as he discovers this correctly, he arrives at a knowledge of the natural law.

Personal man is at the same time a *historical* being. That does not mean simply that he lives in a time sequence and can thus look back on the past and perhaps also have a presentiment of the future. It means primarily that by reason of his self-understanding and experience of the past and present he both can and must plan the future as a truly human future. Is not all moral knowledge, even the knowledge of the situation-conscience, really an active plan of a possible, perhaps the only possible (or so it is understood) truly human realization of a given reality; and, in so far as this realization has not yet been achieved, a plan for the responsibly formed future of man, a plan for his advance—as person-in-world—into the future? As beings in history we cannot adopt a static attitude; we have to be incessantly making plans for the future—the next moment, the next day, the coming years, the future of humanity following on after us. So we must always attend, as our most specific duty, to the development of our own persons, of the human world around us and of the world in the service of mankind. The carrying into effect of such plans, i.e. of the knowledge gained in consequence of certain behaviour as to what at any given time is to be done from the human point of view, leads to experiences which in their turn can make fresh reflection, knowledge and planning possible and necessary. As a historical being man must be unceasingly concerned about the future, he must think about progress, and so—what in fact is the same thing—his concern for 'the knowledge of natural law' has no definitive end.

Natural law—in the sense of natural moral law—cannot thus be regarded as a static quantity and reality. It cannot be preserved in a book as a collection of precepts and commands. Neither can it be read from facts of nature as though God had woven it into them; for all that can be read from the facts of nature are physical data and laws, not moral regulations and commands. The natural moral law is rather to be understood in a dynamic sense; as the ever new and still to be solved problem of being a person of this world. This, however, implies development and progress. Many branches of knowledge of the natural law concerned with human behaviour and conduct will show themselves to be—at any rate substantially—lasting and do not require repeated calling into question. But there are also areas of knowledge where solutions—arrived at by us humans and held as good and right—are open to doubt. Most important of all, completely new questions are constantly arising particularly at a time when man's probing into the facts of nature and their changing character make it possible for him as a result of experience to regard previous answers to questions, which may have been well-intentioned, as in fact basically 'inhuman' and therefore incorrect.

Development of oneself, one's environment and the world always implies probing into the given facts, conquering the bounds of nature's given reality, in other words *artificium* in relation to *natura* understood as the given facts of nature. The invasion of nature, thus understood, the conquering of its limitations, the *artificium*, is an essential part of being human, of humanizing nature's realities, of the transformation of nature into human culture, of the fulfilment of the mandate to be a person in this world; indeed, the *artificium* pertains to man's nature, if one understands nature, not merely in the sense of actuated given reality, but as personal human existence in its totality. Certainly, not every arbitrary invasion, not every arbitrary *artificium* is human culture. The invasion, the *artificium* must be of such an order as to be worthy of man—as a person in nature and the world—and as to create human values—'human' understood in the fullest sense of the word—and not 'non-values'. But whether certain invasions, *artificia*—are to be judged as—in the best sense—'human' or as basically 'inhuman', we will often discern correctly in our first 'draft', i.e. at the first attempt at a moral judgement; but it can also happen that experience leads us sooner or later to revise this draft, our moral pronouncement.

When we regard the natural moral law in its dynamic sense, in other words as the mandate to live as a person of this world, it becomes apparent that this achievement always demands some use of force—taking this word in its widest sense. We have to tear away the secrets and potentialities from this world entrusted to us, have to free it from its fixity and pure reality, have to impose on it our reason and our will. The same holds good of the shaping of human society and humanity. For our task is not simply to protect the given realities—neither the realities of human ignorance or indolence, nor the realities of social order created or evolved in good or ill will; the goal of human society is not its ever existing condition and order, but its ever improving formation—the common good in the best and fullest sense of the word. The fulfilment of this mandate involves a struggle in various ways against much and many—thus the use in some form or other of force. And must we not in order to live in the sense of 'people of this world' constantly force ourselves to rid our minds of ideas, knowledge, customs, which have become too dear to us? The 'fight' for truth and for a better shaping of life and the world has not only to be waged with others, but with ourselves. That which is given, has become, has been formed by us, is also that which in some way has to be overcome because it is to be continued.

III. THE 'MORAL STANDARDIZATION' OF HUMAN PROGRESS

The idea has already been repeatedly expressed that not every type of progress, certainly not every probing into facts 'in the name of progress' is morally justifiable—since it is not 'human' in the fullest sense of the word. But one could well ask: if 'being a person of this world'—in other words progress—constitutes, according to natural law, the task of man in this world, then isn't progress itself the real moral norm of man, so that there is no need to search for moral norms for progress—the development of the 'man in world'? The question is perfectly justifiable. But before we turn expressly to this question let it be said that progress which is effected in opposition to a real moral order is in reality no progress.

If the question is concerned with whether the unjustifiable and accordingly immoral could exist in the realm of development of the man-world reality, a twofold reply is indicated. (a) It would be unjustifiable and thus immoral if man wished to be indifferent to the development of the mankind-world reality, not to concern himself with it. For this would mean that man was not accepting and fulfilling his mandate to be 'a person in the world'. (b) It would be unjustifiable and immoral if man wished to pursue a course of development which was basically only alleged progress. This because man is committed to progress. Here the following should clearly be stated: progress must always be 'human', may never be 'inhuman'. Yet it is a question of the development of the man-world reality. Whoever speaks of progress, of the progress and development of the world in its material aspect, in other words of technical progress, must ultimately mean the progress of man—of human society. The world has no meaning except in its relation to mankind, it only possesses meaning as a world of men. Thus 'inhuman' progress is not in the true and full sense progress; and therefore it is immoral. On the other hand this means that it is immoral to remain indifferent to—true—progress, not to concern oneself with it.

The danger of man serving the cause of spurious development, and thus basically non-development, instead of true progress lies in the concupiscent egoism of man 'of the Fall'. This man can be so fascinated by the possibility of a merely 'partial' and therefore 'inhuman' progress that he disregards mankind to achieve, for example, purely technical progress. The will to progress must withstand the attempt to exclude man and to overlook the question of whether a particular development is worthy of man and will be of service to him.

The second of the principles mentioned for the morality of human progress poses the question of whether we can establish more concrete principles to indicate more closely just what man desirous of progress must heed, what he may aspire to and what not, what means cannot be employed to achieve a progress worthy of man, what calculated dangers and consequences he may not take on himself, and more in this vein. In short, have we knowledge of moral principles which—apart from the basic requirement that man must concern himself with progress and indeed with 'human' progress in the full sense—in some way regulate the active progress of the man-world reality and confine it within certain bounds? Obviously this question is identical with the general question concerning the possibility of moral principles for human conduct in general.

This means repeating the thesis often expressed today, that there are very few moral principles which make purely *a priori*—in the strongest sense of the term, and in this sense metaphysical—assertions concerning man's moral conduct as such. They relate primarily to man's personal, responsible, social and historical nature which, as in all human behaviour, demands consideration in the realization of his mandate and desire for progress. These general moral principles are of considerable importance and have their consequences in all human conduct, but alone they scarcely produce concrete guide-lines for human behaviour and human progress. More concrete guide-lines presuppose experience and knowledge

o

of concrete reality and its possible method of realization—
together with the consequences. This experience of and
information about the man-world reality which is constantly changing because of its achievements and experience—experience of the past, present and the immediate
future—lead us continually to raise afresh the question of the
true humanity and worth in human terms of our action and
progress.

Some considerable problems follow from this which—at
least as problems—must be looked at. Can it be perhaps that
in some areas of human action and behaviour several truly
human solutions are possible—not merely as a result of
erroneous judgement and assessment, but in truth and
objectively? Is it perhaps conceivable that, in different
cultures by reason of a different context and a partly different
scale of values, slightly differing norms of behaviour develop
and indeed—justifiably in this context—must develop? Can
we perhaps say that an ideal of human conduct which presupposes a certain level of culture and a certain scale of
values at a certain time in history cannot be regarded as the
optimum in behaviour when this culture level is not reached
and the corresponding scale of values not comprehended?
Take, for instance, many of our present-day pronouncements
on the correct social relationship between man and woman—
whether in Europe or America: were not these still regarded
at the turn of the century as to some extent neither judicious
nor acceptable? And on the other hand are not the pronouncements of the Apostle Paul on this relationship (e.g.
the subordinate position of woman in society) to some extent
unacceptable to us and therefore of no account?

There can be no doubt that man can know, or by working
can arrive at, more concrete principles and guide-lines for the
way to his—truly human—progress. Yet new experiences
and reflection on these can never put man once and for all
in complete possession of all guide-lines and principles, down
to the smallest detail, with no further need for change. For
man seeking progress must continue to look for and discover

certain principles concerning the humanity of his progress, in other words moral principles.

Anyone wanting to achieve progress has to plan the future. It is often not possible to assess in advance with complete certainty the consequences for the future of certain projects, whether in the field of social work, hygiene, economics, space-research etc. Here imperatives[2] must be laid down of which one cannot say with certainty that they are the right ones, i.e. that they will prove in the long run to be worthy of man and therefore morally justifiable. Man committed and bound to progress can and must, if he wants to comply with his existence as a 'being of progress', have the will to adopt courageous and at the same time intelligently worked out imperatives. Experience and foresight, a look at the goal, means and possible consequences allow one to arrive at a sufficiently safe judgement as to whether the attempt at a step forward, and thus a necessity, is humanly-morally defensible. While the combination of courage and intelligence in the drawing up of imperatives does not permit man to shrink back from the risk attached to taking a step forward in the not completely discernible future, it leads him to take care to see that the attempted step proves to be true human progress. A complete rationalization of the assent to or rejection of an imperative or even the superiority of one imperative over another is often not feasible. The better someone knows the totality of the reality implied in the imperative and the deeper and more genuine his human image, the more fit he will be for an imperative of true human progress.

The Church, too, will constantly find herself in the situation either of setting herself concrete imperatives—e.g. in the encyclical *Populorum Progressio*—or of judging imperatives already laid down or in the process of being laid down by

[2]Cf. K. Rahner, 'Prinzipien und Imperative' in: *Das Dynamische in der Kirche*, Freiburg i. Br. 1958, 14–37.

certain persons or groups. In this field she will more often give pastoral guidance than teaching magisterial. Since such imperatives often presuppose a high level of knowledge in various profane sciences, it would be better for the official Church to be cautious on these questions[3]—in so far as they lie outside her field of operation. Politics, sociology, technology, biology and much besides are, however, not the field of competence of the Church—even if these fields are as open to those who make up the Church as to other men. Indeed in so far as the Church and the true believing Christian have a view of mankind—a view which in faith and under the dynamics of faith has become freed and is truly *human*—and correspondingly an understanding of the 'humanity' of imperatives, they are called to a say in the judgement of imperatives governing human progress.[4]

IV. PROGRESS AND THE DYNAMIC UNDERSTANDING OF MORALITY

A proper understanding and moral evaluation of progress depends in no small measure upon a proper understanding of moral concepts and principles. At the same time it is of decisive importance whether one is dealing with a mainly static or a truly dynamic interpretation. Only by overcoming a one-sided, static way of thinking, by the ability to think dynamically in the moral field, can one find the way to a moral understanding of human progress. Here I would like —by way of example—to set out the significance of the

---

[3]Cf. K. Rahner, 'Theologische Reflexionen zum Problem der Säkularisation', in *Schriften zur Theologie*, VIII, 637–66.

[4]K. Rahner speaks of a 'moral instinct of faith' ('moralischen Glaubensinstinkt'). E. Schillebeeckx interprets in a similar way the words of the Constitution *Gaudium et Spes* (art. 46), that we recognize what we ought to do 'in the light of the gospel and of human experience'. See K. Rahner, 'Zum Problem der genetischen Manipulation', in *Schriften zur Theologie*, VIII, 303 f. and E. Schillebeeckx, 'The Magisterium and the World of Politics', *Concilium* (4) 1968, 12–21.

dynamic interpretation of certain moral principles for the understanding of human progress. This will be followed by a short reflection on the relationship of progress and force.

1. The principle of totality means, in traditional moral theology, that the part is at the service of the whole and may therefore be sacrificed in its service—at least in so far as this whole represents a unity of being and not merely a working unity. This principle has often been understood in a one-sided, static way. Thus it is said that part of the whole may be sacrificed in order to keep the whole in being or in health and strength, or to restore it to this condition by averting a present injury or an imminent danger. A dynamic conception of the same principle would assert that a part may be sacrificed in order to bring about the development of the whole beyond its static givenness, in order to achieve the development of its latent possibilities. And this is progress.

Some examples may illustrate this point. Moral theology never put any difficulties in a doctor's way when it was a question of removing an inflamed appendix. The diseased part could be removed in order to save the organism as a whole from the danger that threatened it and so to preserve it in its given state. On the other hand, if it was a question of removing a healthy appendix which did not threaten the condition of the entire organism either directly or indirectly, then objections were raised. Even reference to the anticipatory elimination of an eventual future danger which could perhaps—above all in special circumstances, for example, the absence of medical help—prove fatal, even this was not sufficient. It was not admitted that this kind of medical removal of a part (the appendix) could be justified as treatment required by the organism as a whole, and therefore as a step forward.

A number of theoreticians and practitioners have now changed their view. For instance, an operation for aesthetic purposes—on the face of it an interference and to that extent a 'sacrifice'—does not serve the preservation or restoration to health of the whole, but signifies an 'improvement' of the whole beyond its given state. Accordingly, objections were raised to such an operation on the basis of a solely 'static' understanding of the principle of totality. If, however, on the other hand, a person was suffering psychologically from his disfigurement, then intervention was allowed in order to free him from his psychological illness, that is, in the interest of the health of the whole. But why should not an intervention for the 'improvement' of the whole, for appropriate reasons, i.e. for the sake of progress, be justified as rational and, therefore, moral? In that case the principle of totality would be understood dynamically, not statically. At the present time, and in the near future, new possibilities seem to be opening up. Our aim increasingly is to influence and control the biological reality and structure of mankind. May one or may one not make use of these possibilities which, by and large, are intended to promote the qualitative improvement of man rather than preserve him in his existing state and cure him of his ills? That will depend largely upon the question of the conditions for realizing these possibilities and the long-term risks of such interference. The basic question, however, is whether the principle of totality is to be understood only in a static sense—preservation and healing of the whole—or also dynamically. A progressively deepening understanding of this principle, and the conception of human morality (natural law) expounded above, justify its dynamic understanding and application in the service of progress, rightly understood.

There is a principle of law and morality that in doubtful cases favours the fortunate party in possession: *in dubio, melior est condicio possidentis;* when in doubt, the legal presumption favours the actual possessor. The principle that legal certainty must be guaranteed in the community tends in the same direction. Both have led, and easily do lead, people to be inclined to look for law and justice—and consequently 'the will of God'—on the side of the actual order of things. But this betrays static thinking. Basically, however, it is a question neither of the existing order as such, nor of some other order, but of the just order which has continually to be sought for, planned and put into effect. Alongside the principles of legal certainty and the preferment of the actual possessor there must stand this other, more dynamic principle, namely that our real task is always to seek the better order of things. Only by reference to this other, dynamic principle can both the aforesaid principles be properly understood. Conversely, dynamism would turn to revolution and disorder if it did not have regard to the importance of legal presumption and legal certainty. The desire for progress, which seeks always to create a better and more just order, is only truly human, and progressive in the real sense, if the static elements of legal presumption and legal certainty are properly regarded. On the other hand, regard for legal presumption and certainty becomes anti-progressive and thus 'inhuman' if it overlooks the necessary drive towards an even better order.

As the re-orientation from a static to a more dynamic way of thinking proceeds, it affects, for example, the evaluation of revolution.[5] Towards the end of the last and the beginning of the present century, both in the writings of theologians and in the documents of the Church, there prevailed the thesis, illustrating a static way of thinking, that revolution, as a violent overthrow of a given order, was a violation of law, contrary to justice, and therefore immoral. Only if, later on, the new order brought about by the revolution could not be reversed without great disadvantage to the common good, did it thereby become legitimate. This thesis has now changed. If the common good can retrospectively legitimize the new order, then this is tantamount to admitting

---

[5] Cf. R. Hauser, *Autoritat und Macht. Die stratlische Autoritat in der neuen protestantischen und in der Catholischen Gesellschaftslehre*, Heidelberg 1949.

that it is not the actual existence as such of a particular order that gives it legitimacy, but the more dynamic requirement of the common good. But in that case the possibility cannot be excluded that an actually existing order might prove unjust from the point of view of the common good, and that its preservation would therefore depend on unjust force. This means, however, that the enforced introduction of a new order will not necessarily be legitimized only in retrospect, but also on occasion in advance—though naturally only as a last resort and on condition of a tolerable relationship between the ills of revolution and its anticipated success. Pius XII made this teaching his own in his letter of 28 March 1937 to the Mexican bishops.[6]

The example cited in itself explains how in many other questions also the right way, that is the way of (true) progress, is to be found not by a one-sided, static assessment of the actual state of affairs, but by a dynamic outlook on the more correct and better solution. Without this dynamic outlook neither the mastery of situations of social injustice nor the decolonization of peoples capable of free self-determination would be possible, so long as a one-sided, static view insisted on the—formal—rights of the existing order. To say this is not to say what kind of means may be applied for the alteration of the actual situation in given circumstances.

That the rights of the dynamic will to progress, as against static rigidity, can also be of importance in the Church is understood today even by those who do not wish to speak of this question or are actually afraid of it. The fact of a hierarchical authority established in the Church by Christ does not necessarily stand in opposition to the dynamic will to progress in the ecclesiastical community. For the Church, as a human society, despite the hierarchical authority established within it, is not exempted from the laws of social life, above all the law of the primacy of the common good. A brief example can be given. If in the field of positive law

---

[6]Denz.-Schönm., *Enchiridion*, 3775 s.

there exists *epikeia*, as the virtue of a superior sense of justice,[7] then this virtue also has its importance in the ecclesiastical community and in relation to the order established by its hierarchical authority. To be sure, it is easier for *epikeia* to permit or require a responsible action not corresponding to the letter of ecclesiastical order in the private than the public sphere. But an action based on *epikeia* is not fundamentally excluded in the public field either. If one follows up this line of thought consistently, then pressure and action on behalf of an alteration of the established order cannot, basically, be absolutely and in every case unjust. Clearly, firm action to replace the good by the better for the sake of progress, motivated by a correct understanding of the common good, must also have a place in the Church. The Spirit of the Lord, and the understanding of reality in this Spirit, are not absolutely reserved to Church authority. Of course, great delicacy and a high gift of discrimination will be needed to establish the right relation between willing and respectful readiness to obey on the one hand, and on the other, zeal in the service of progress on behalf of the people of God. When the matter is looked at in this way, it is as true of *epikeia* as of the will to progress that it can only be properly put into practice by a person of true competence, great sense of responsibility, and humble readiness to serve.

Moral theology is accustomed to distinguish between negative commands, i.e. prohibitions, and affirmative commands, i.e. precepts. So far as prohibitions are concerned, they are not only always valid, but have to be respected on every occasion. Precepts, on the other hand, while always valid, do not have to be carried out on every occasion: *praecepta negativa valent semper et pro semper, praecepta affirmativa valent semper sed non pro semper*. The meaning is clear. A prohibition may not be disregarded but an action cannot always be commanded. One does not constantly have to

[7]Thomas Aquinas, *S. Theol.* II–II 120, 2 ad 1.

smile at one's neighbour, give alms to all the poor without distinction, and renounce every justified action that might possibly cause annoyance to someone else. Let us now consider the meaning of that part of the principle that reads: *praecepta affirmativa valent semper sed non pro semper*. It expresses the precept that one must put into practice the values involved in these commands, but that this putting into practice has to be co-ordinated with the realization of other values, that is to say that the best combination of values must be discovered and put into effect. The values whose realization is under discussion are in the first place only relative values, *bona physica*, not absolute values, *bona moralia*. To smile at one's neighbour, to give alms, to avoid distressing one's neighbour—these are human values, but only relative values. To put them into practice is *often* appropriate or necessary, but not *always*—the latter applies only to absolute values, *bona moralia*. Thus the principle we are discussing really means this: there is an absolute moral duty to put into practice *in the best possible manner* the values indicated in affirmative commands, that is to say with regard to other equally necessary values. This expresses the basic precept of human morality. In this world we have an absolute duty to make the best possible effort towards the realization of (relative) values. What this 'best possible' is, what the best possible realization of the man-world reality can be, today and tomorrow, this mankind has to find out for itself. But this search for the best possible concrete solution itself forms part of the absolute moral precept, to make the best that is possible out of the man-world reality. The principle, *praecepta affirmativa valent semper sed non pro semper,* is therefore to be understood dynamically, and means in the last analysis that man, in building the man-world reality, is bound constantly to build for the betterment of the world, that is, to progress.

2. There are other moral principles to be examined for their dynamic meaning and corresponding relationship to

human progress. What follows, however, comprises an enquiry into another link between progress and the dynamic interpretation of morality—the relationship between progress on the one hand, and power and force on the other. For the realization of the best that is possible, i.e. progress, in the last analysis permits of no *quieta non movere* but requires the application of power and force. Progress has continually to be extracted anew from static given reality, and this comes about by the dynamic of power and force legitimized by progress.

Nature only yields its secrets, its latent powers and laws, its as yet unexplored and unrealized possibilities, if man with his mind and will and the powers they control wrenches them loose by power and force, to make them his own. Progress, however, requires man to confront in all kinds of ways, with power and force, not only nature, which is not free, but also free humanity itself. To be sure, progress can only be genuine, i.e. genuine human progress, if it is attained by an exercise of power and force that is *humanly justified*.

Even the upbringing of children is, in a sense, an exercise of power. Children are not simply left to themselves but are given into the superior power of adults. They may not and cannot develop in unfettered freedom but come, under the 'power-ful' influence of adults and only thus, to human development—in knowledge, ability, conviction and right conduct. The actual or intended influence of social groups on the opinions and behaviour of many individuals is a true exercise of power, without which the progress of humanity would be impossible. The direction of the community by the state, its deliverance from individualistic thinking and behaviour, its guidance along lines of co-operation for public order and the common good, the systematic cultivation of a necessary public opinion (without suppression of the right to legitimate information) are also exercises in power that are aimed at achieving the best that is possible. But such power becomes compulsion if, culpably or not, individuals do not fit into the right and necessary order, and even set themselves against it. Or if, following the egoism embodied in the preservation of the *status quo*, they oppose necessary social reforms. Or if, on the other hand, from the same egoism, they work for upheaval and disorder, which prevent *real* progress. The state, too, stands at the service of the best that is possible by way of progress, and it cannot give this service without the exercise of power and force (cf. *Rom.* 13:1–7).[8]

There also exists, of course, an objectively unjust, and at the same time in many ways subjectively egoistic, exercise of power and force, which gives itself out as acting in the service of progress. Such progress is 'inhuman' and therefore only an apparent progress, in fact it is a lack of progress. Where objectives are aimed at or methods applied (for ends just in themselves) with power and force—which is unworthy of humanity and therefore 'inhuman'—there progress does not really exist. Slavery—whatever the 'lofty' objectives in view—can in our society only be seen as an instance of the unjust use of force. Equally, the enforced maintenance, by

[8]The problem of violence versus non-violence demands careful treatment. In the present situation violence is usually understood in the narrow sense as an attack on a person's life and limb. This is so despite the fact that there are many other forms of violence against persons which can be even more damaging to individuals or groups or society as a whole than an attack on life and limb (cf. 1. above).

Quite often today non-violence is proposed as an absolute (human or Christian) imperative, and the use of force (above all in the sense of an attack on life and limb) as an absolute prohibition. Apart from the fact that this does not accord with traditional Christian teaching (cf. the doctrines of justified self-defence, of 'just war' and justifiable death penalty), there seems here to be an inaccurate idea of the related concepts of 'absolute' and 'relative' values in the moral field. Love and justice are moral, that is, *absolute* values (*bona moralia*) which, as such, may never be violated. The use of force involves an action that violates a *relative* human value, and accordingly inflicts a *malum physicum*. Even the preservation or the taking of life are not, in themselves, an absolute value or an absolute evil, else it would not be permissible in any circumstances to kill or allow to die—and this is contrary to all tradition. Only a correct assessment of advantage, an assessment of the various values and evils implicit in an action (abstract or concrete) makes it possible to establish an absolute. In practice, moral theology has always applied this principle, for example to the question of what relevant values justify the killing of a man (e.g. capital punishment). This does not only apply to an action with a double effect, that is, the case in

whatever means, of a *status quo* where social equality is inadequate is, objectively, an unjust exercise of power and force. It can be classified as lack of (human) progress, even though it may allow for partial progress. The manipulation of public opinion by false information or by the unlawful prevention of a free flow of information, the non-safeguarding of personal rights, the enforcement of objectives by the dictatorial exercise of power—none of these serve progress in a way appropriate to human dignity, and they therefore do not contribute to a truly 'human' progress. It may be that in special circumstances, and for a temporary period, this kind of use of power and force is the only way to realize the good of necessary progress. A correct judgement on this presupposes a high level of knowledge of the issues, a deep

---

which the relative human evil, e.g. injury or death, is brought about freely and consciously, without this evil being the motive of the action.

The Sermon on the Mount does not teach non-violence as an absolute imperative; but rather, it does teach the absolute imperatives of love and justice. As these in certain circumstances, taking into account the balance of the implied (relative) values and evils, may require the renunciation of force, the readiness for such renunciation is necessarily implied in the absolute value of love and justice. But concrete ways of behaving which the Sermon on the Mount prescribes, are to be understood rather as 'ethical models', as is shown not only by the hyperbolic style of expression but also by the behaviour of Christ (for example, his self-defence before the court).

If it is said that non-violence is more in accord with the gospel than the use of violence, that is in a certain sense true, but should not be wrongly understood. For the gospel does not absolutely exclude the use of force in the world of the Fall. The absolute command of love may even require the use of force. Of course, force is then not an ideal but the best that is possible. For where it is a symptom of the Fall, i.e. of the sin that has entered into this world, there it has to be reckoned as something that, in the field of the possible (the calculation of advantage), must in this sinful world increasingly be made superfluous. But so long as this possibility does not actually exist, the use of force remains a possible expression of love and justice as an absolute precept.

It would therefore be wrong to say that the 'just' use of force was nothing but the application of the principle that 'the end justifies the means'. Something could also be said about this principle. The following must suffice here: in this principle 'means' signifies a *malum absolutum* (*morale*). If the use of force were absolutely, i.e. morally, bad, it would obviously never qualify as a justifiable means in the fallen world. But it is precisely this assertion that has been questioned above.

understanding of the dignity of the human person, and great consciousness of responsibility.

A use of power and force that is unjustified, because it does not really serve the cause of 'human' progress, cannot be in the interests of man's duty and will to progress—that is a tautology. There remains the question of how the justified use of power and force is to be more precisely understood. A few comments are offered here. *Certain*—not all—justified exercises of power and force on behalf of progress stand as signs of the sin that has entered into this world, and their justification or necessity therefore makes visible the real condition of the fallen man-world reality. All who do not subscribe, as far as they are able, to the best possible progressive realization of man, his society and his world, or who actually resist it out of personal egoism or the blindness that springs from the fundamental egoism of fallen man, act sinfully in so far as they do this. On the other hand, power and force used in the service of real progress are not in themselves sinful, but are a defence against objectively unjust and perhaps also subjectively egoistical and sinful behaviour, and in any case a defence against 'the sins of the world', and their consequences. But if the use of force can be justified, its relation to the sinful condition of the world should not be overlooked. From this it follows that we are always bound so to change the world's condition that the application of force, which is a sign of the world's sinfulness, will become increasingly unnecessary.

V. THE RELIGIOUS AND MORAL CHARACTER OF HUMAN PROGRESS

We began by examining the problems which caused moral theology to arrive only with difficulty at a correct moral and religious assessment of human progress. Seen as a purely natural, purely secular, purely immanent value, progress seems to be in competition with the absolute values of morality, religion and the supernatural. So far we have tried to indicate the place of human progress in the moral field. In conclusion, we shall briefly investigate the moral and religious character of human progress by means of a summing up and a theological continuation of the foregoing observations. This leads to an evaluation substantially different from that conditioned by the difficulties mentioned above.

It is interesting to note that people have been more ready to regard as morally valuable the healing of the sick, for example, or the support of the needy, than human progress in the sense of the active development of the man-world reality. And yet both these activities are 'moral' in *the same sense*. In themselves, it is true, they are only *relative* values. But their proper and meaningful realization is part of man's moral and therefore *absolute* duty. Progress is not merely a physical possibility, and not merely a morally unobjectionable exercise, but a moral duty. That should be plain enough from the preceding exposition.

The turning to the world expressed in the will to progress is, since the Fall, in permanent danger of running away into a secret or open egoism. The Son of God made man has brought to this world the new man of the kingdom of God, in whom the Spirit conquers egoism. Despite the Fall, the world has once and for all been taken up by God, through the sending of his Son. The positive application to the reality of man and his world and their development, that is progress, does not simply belong to the task of creation but also to the expression of God's will and the commission entrusted to men in the sending to them of his Son. God's turning to the world in the incarnation and self-giving of his Son carries with it the task of accepting and bringing progressively to development God's creation, that is, man and his world. This is part of the realization of God's incarnation in this world.

At the same time the development of reality that is man

and his world, in other words progress, is not to be seen as something that has nothing to do with the supernatural and with grace. For the bond of supernatural, grace-given life between the Father and those who are taken up into the divine community of love, does not exist in isolation from man in the world, but is indeed man's true life. This true life of community of grace with the Father is fulfilled in and through the immanent formation of the reality of the world. But this forward-moving world-formation is already something more than itself, more than a purely immanent, intra-worldly happening.

It has already been pointed out that one can make the immanence of world-formation, and of progress, into an absolute and thus misunderstand it, that one can be hypno-tized by the immanent possibilities and take to egoistical sham-progress, that is, 'inhumanity', instead of to 'human' progress. Grace, faith and love make fallen man open to real progress. Thus grace, faith and love enter into progress and it becomes itself a sign of grace working for faith and love in the world. We are not raising the question of how this takes place in Christians and non-Christians, in just men and in sinners. But if true progress is only possible if the man under grace constantly detaches himself and, by power and force, others also, from egoism, then the active realization and development of the man-world reality, that is to say progress, is always signed with the cross. A will to progress that is absolutely opposed to this sign ultimately makes for inhuman progress, non-progress. It does not make way for the power of Christ transforming man through grace. It resists that immanent formation of the world in and through which the mission of the incarnate Son is to be completed. But where progress takes place under the influence of grace, and under the sign of the cross, there it is able to bring about the true formation of 'man-in-the-world' as this is intended by our creation and salvation. At the same time the continuing immanent formation of the world leads to an increase in human freedom, in so far as the world, in its continuing formation, offers less resistance to the realization of the 'new life' of the Christian as he lives it in the midst of the world.[9]

In this way true progress becomes the expression and sign of the eschatological salvation that is already present and is also drawing ever closer to us.

[9]Thus a free renunciation, for example voluntary poverty, does not contradict the commandment of human progress. For a free renunciation, as witnessing hope in the transforming power of grace upon the destructive egoism of fallen man, has the prophetic mission in the world of warning men against the danger of an inhuman 'progress', and pointing to the principle of all progress which is that it has to be the progress of *man*, of *humanity*. Renunciation and poverty do not constitute a value *as such* and indeed would have to be considered as obstacles to progress if fallen man did not continually feel and experience his own egoism and were unable to hope for its overcoming—a process which only the Christian can understand as 'fall' and 'redemption' by grace. If man is to progress in the world, two things are needed, depending on the individual's vocation—active participation in the world, and renunciation of the world. Only thus will it be possible for man's progress to be truly 'human.'

253

(Copy)